GRAPHIC SURVIVAL STORIES

DEFYING DEATH IN THE JUNGLE

by Gary Jeffrey

illustrated by Terry Riley

rosen publishing's rosen central

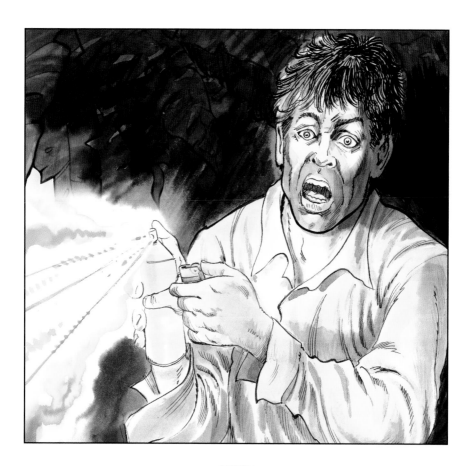

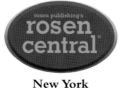

New York

Published in 2010 by The Rosen Publishing Group, Inc.
29 East 21st Street, New York, NY 10010

Designed and produced by
David West Books

Editor: Katharine Pethick

Photo credits:
4t, Martin St-Amant; 4r, LollyKnit; 4b, yimhafiz; 5m, themanzomandisastersquadron;
5b, 5Julien Harneis; 6-7, Will Ellis; 6l, 6r, Antoine Hubert; 6b, cliff1066; 45t,
DeusXFlorida

Library of Congress Cataloging-in-Publication Data

Jeffrey, Gary.
 Defying death in the jungle / Gary Jeffrey, illustrated by Terry Riley.
    p. cm.
 Includes index.
 ISBN 978-1-4358-3529-0 (library binding) -- ISBN 978-1-61532-861-1 (pbk.) -- ISBN
978-1-61532-862-8 (6-pack)
 1. Jungle survival. 2. Survival skills. I. Title.
 GV200.5.J45 2010
 613.69--dc22

                                    2009037673

Manufactured in China

CPSIA Compliance Information: Batch #DW0102YA:
For Further Information contact Rosen Publishing, New York, New York at 1-800-237-9932

CONTENTS

THE WORLD'S JUNGLES

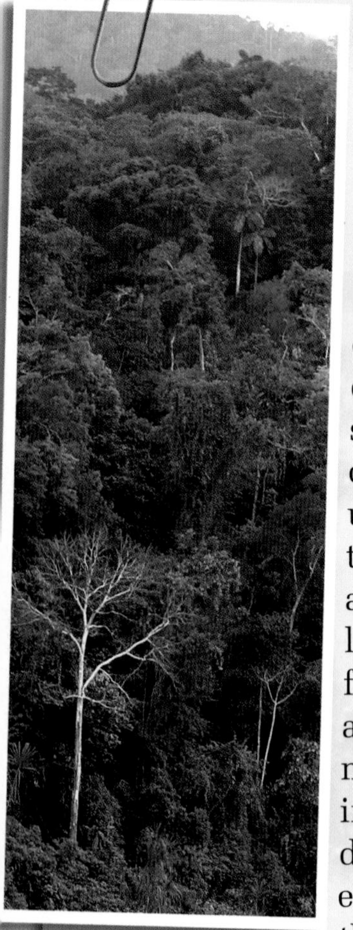

The Amazon rainforest

A jungle is a wild, overgrown area of forest. There are many kinds of natural forest environments around the world, but the most extreme type of jungle is tropical rainforest.

HOT AND WET

Spread along the equator, tropical rainforests exist in a continuous, rainy summer. Canopies of broadleaf and evergreen trees, pierced by soaring ancient giant trees, cloak the land. The canopy and under-canopy thrive with plant, animal, and insect life. On the forest floor, fallen leaves and other plant matter rot rapidly in the gloom, their decay fueling the endless growth of the forest.

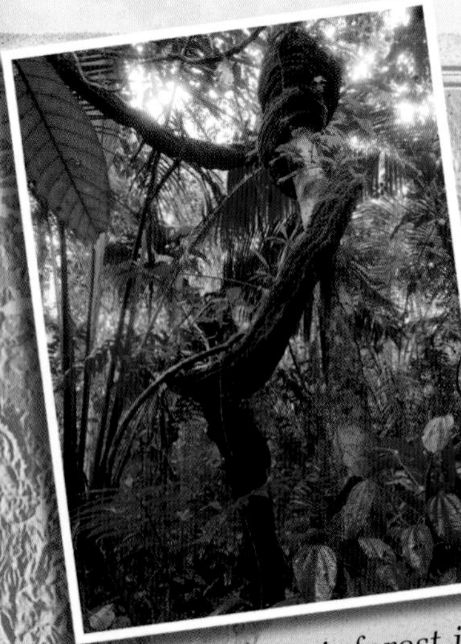

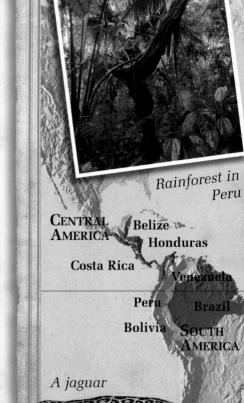

Rainforest in Peru

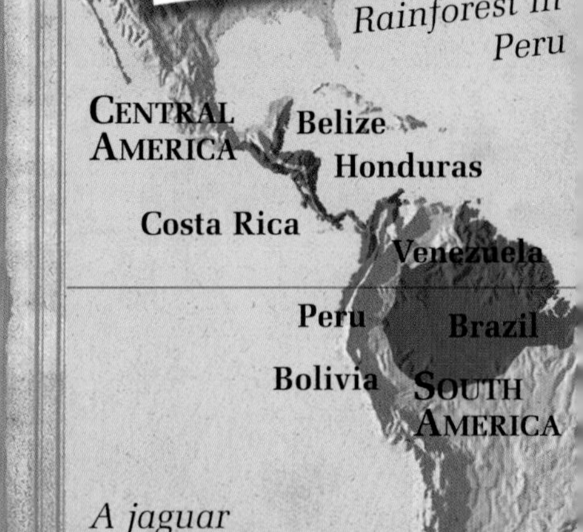
CENTRAL AMERICA
Belize
Honduras
Costa Rica
Venezuela
Peru
Brazil
Bolivia
SOUTH AMERICA

BIODIVERSITY

Eagles, butterflies, bats, and monkeys live in the topmost layer of the rainforest. Most of the food in a rainforest is held below, in the canopy layer, where snakes, toucans, and tree frogs are found. The under-canopy has large-leaved shrubs and is home to jaguars, red-eyed tree frogs, and leopards. Anteaters and insects dominate the forest floor.

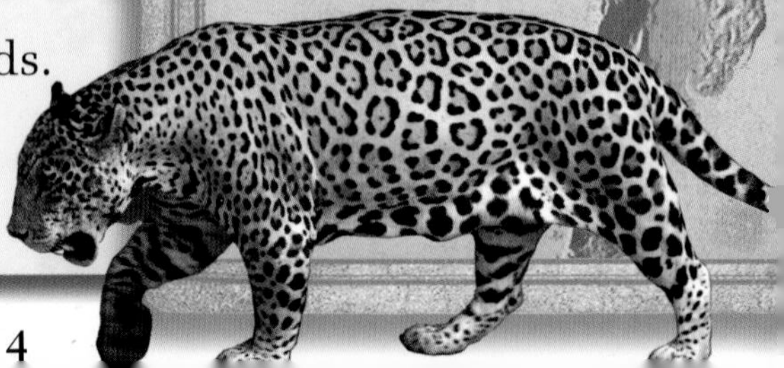

A jaguar

Rainforest People

Although rainforests are thought to hold more than half of all Earth's species, they are not a habitat fit for humans. Tribes that make a home in the jungle have to clear the land and farm its relatively poor soil. They can only use the forest for game, fruits, and plants. These are the very elements that make rainforests compelling places to explore.

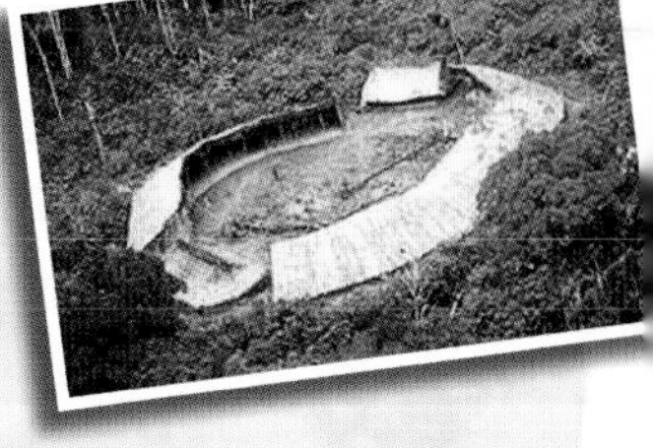

A native settlement sits in a clearing of South American rainforest.

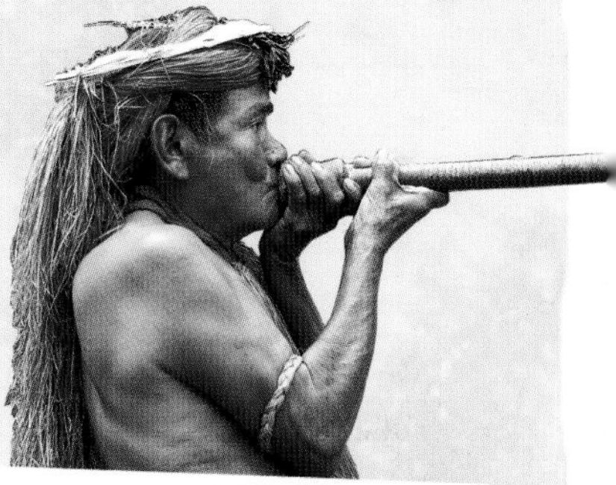

A Peruvian tribesman uses a blowgun.

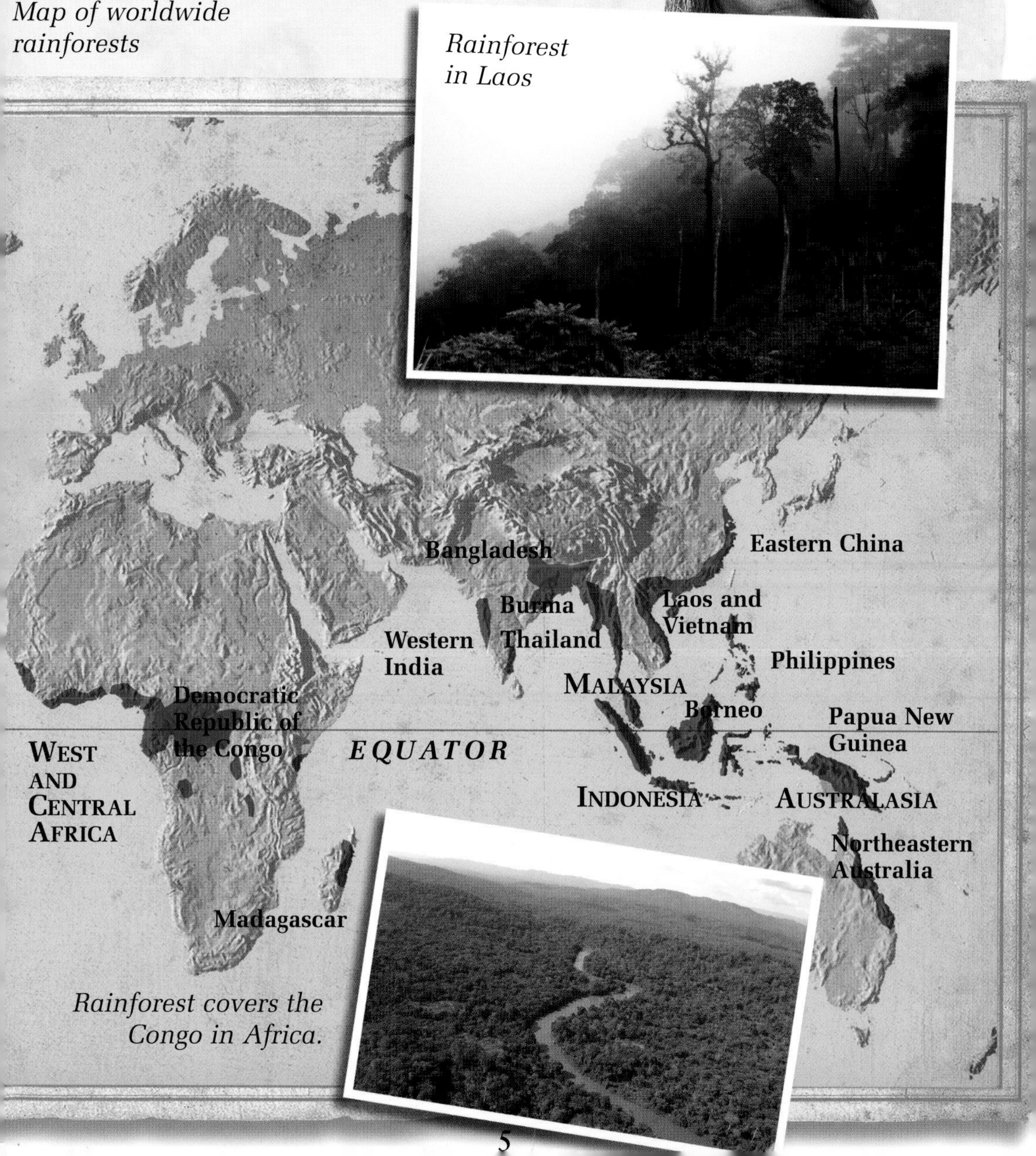

Bangladesh
Eastern China
Burma
Laos and Vietnam
Western India
Thailand
Philippines
Malaysia
Democratic Republic of the Congo
Borneo
Papua New Guinea
West and Central Africa
EQUATOR
Indonesia
Australasia
Northeastern Australia
Madagascar

Map of worldwide rainforests

Rainforest in Laos

Rainforest covers the Congo in Africa.

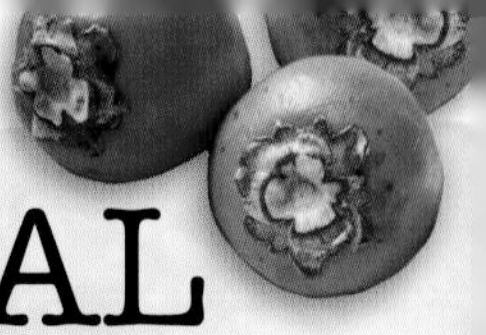

JUNGLE SURVIVAL

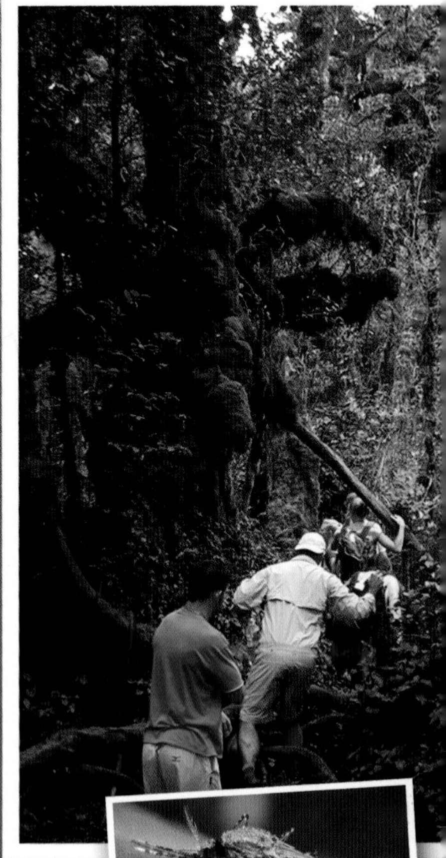

Jungles are some of the most amazing places to visit. However, caution is required. Their extreme climate and abundance of life means they can easily become a hostile environment for humans.

Climate Challenge

Although the jungle is wet, it is also hot. Dehydration occurs when you sweat more water than you take in, leading to an illness called heatstroke. The constant humidity (up to 100%) causes wounds to become infected. It also causes fungal infestation on the skin.

Jungle Critters

Although large jungle beasts like leopards, jaguars, and warthogs are fearsome, they are rare. Tiny creatures are the real killers. Insects like the blood-sucking mosquito carry malaria (the most deadly disease in human history). Snake bites, scorpion stings, attacks from fire ants, and infected leech bites can quickly turn a healthy adventurer into a casualty if left untreated.

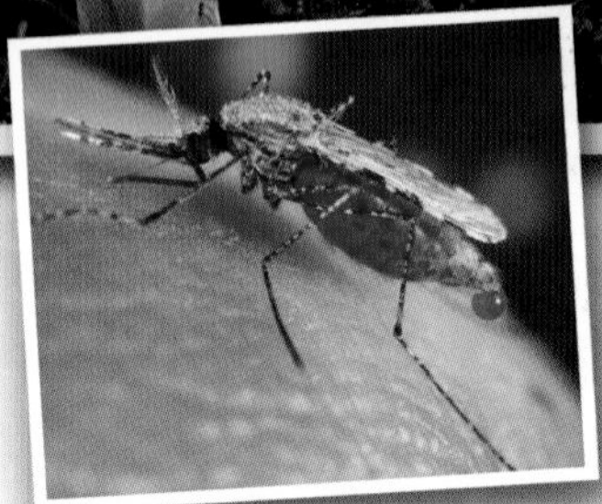

A malarial mosquito

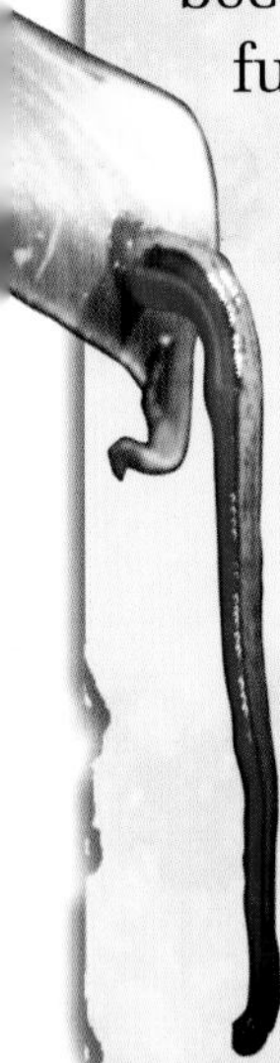

A jungle leech

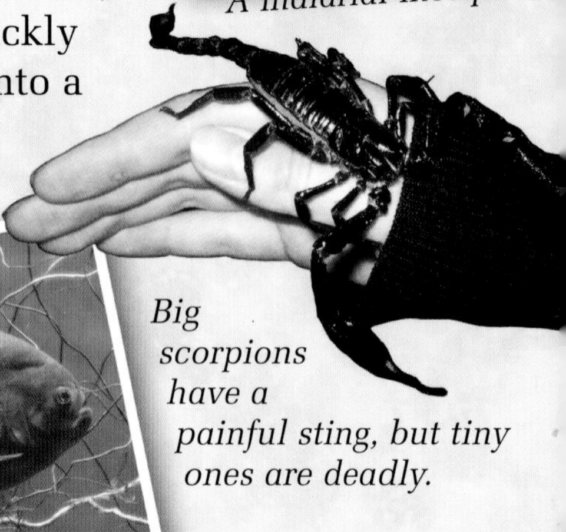

Big scorpions have a painful sting, but tiny ones are deadly.

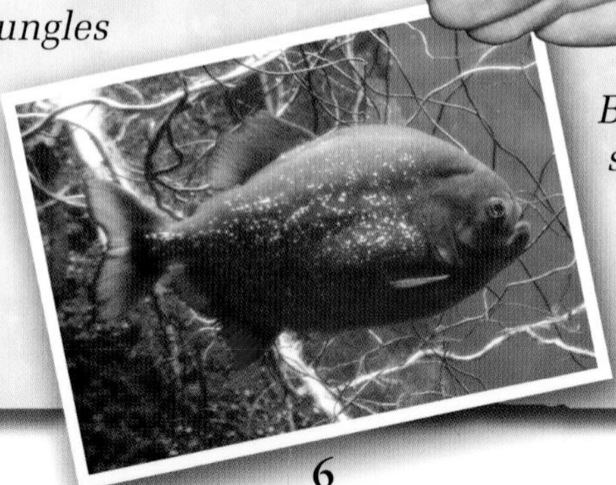

Piranhas from the jungles of South America are dangerous, but anacondas, alligators, and crocodiles are more deadly.

Hidden Dangers

The most common cause of death in the rainforest is falling trees. Trees that are in a continuous cycle of growth and decay often drop timber. Microscopic organisms are also a deadly hazard. Parasites and unusual diseases are present in all but the freshest of water, which must always be treated before drinking.

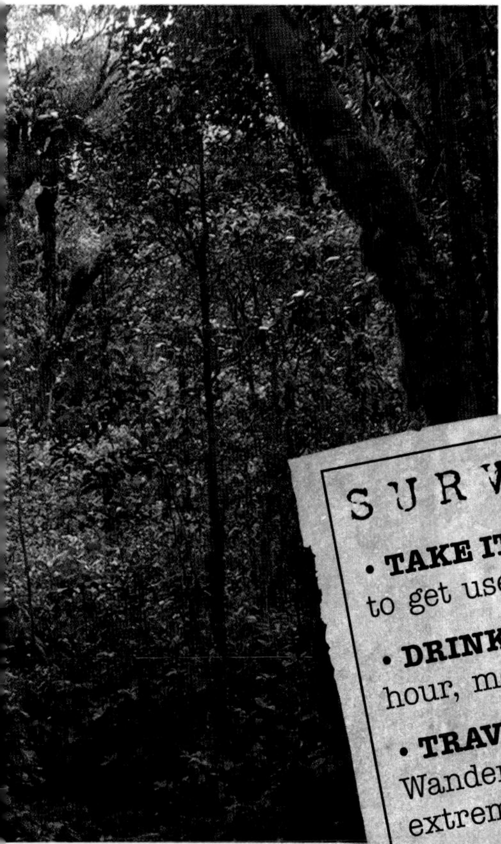

Beware of pulling on jungle vines, and don't camp under an obviously dead tree.

SURVIVAL TIPS

- **TAKE IT EASY.** It can take two weeks to get used to a jungle climate.
- **DRINK LOTS OF WATER** every half hour, more often if you are active.
- **TRAVEL BEFORE NIGHTFALL.** Wandering in the jungle at night is extremely dangerous.
- **SLEEP ABOVE THE GROUND** in a hammock slung between trees.
- **CHECK INSIDE BOOTS AND KEEP POCKETS ZIPPED** against creepy crawlies who like to live inside.
- **DON'T GO SWIMMING ALONE.** There might be dangerous creatures in the water.
- **IF YOU DO GET LOST**, go in one direction until you hit a stream. Go downstream until you find a river, then a bigger river, until you find people.

Natural Resources

In the jungle there are many things to help, as well as hinder, survival. There is lots of firewood and an amazing variety of edible fruits, although these can be difficult to get to. Easier to reach are the vast numbers of bugs that swarm the forest floor. Avoid anything very hairy, brightly colored, or found feeding off dead animals, and you will have a tasty snack.

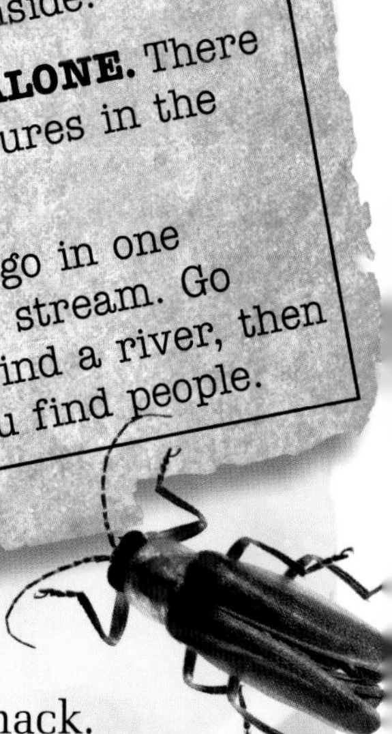

JOURNEY UP THE POISONED RIVER

English Adventurer Colonel Percy Harrison Fawcett

Jungle of the Rio Verde, Bolivia, South America, 1908

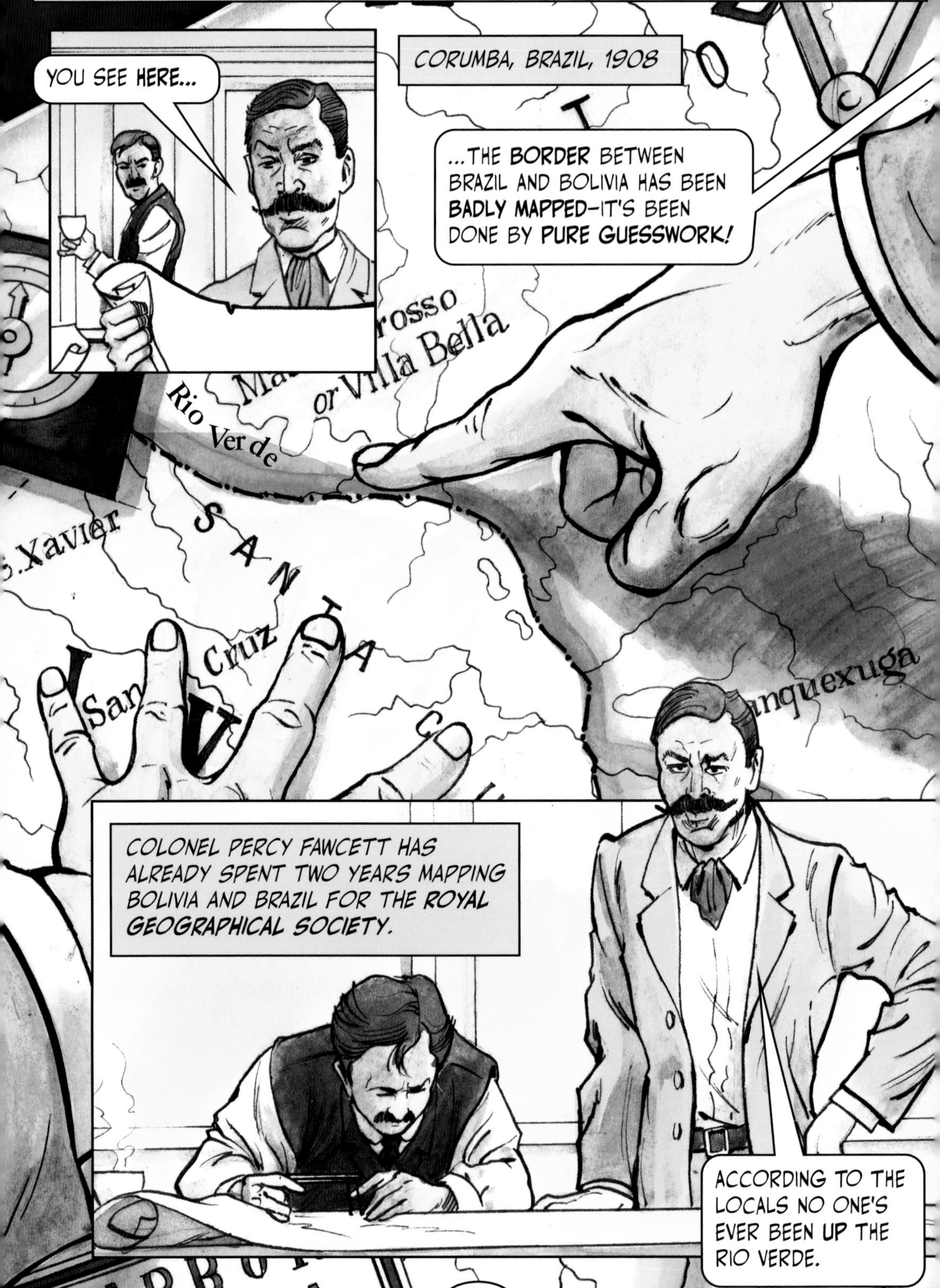

CORUMBA, BRAZIL, 1908
YOU SEE HERE...
...THE BORDER BETWEEN BRAZIL AND BOLIVIA HAS BEEN BADLY MAPPED—IT'S BEEN DONE BY PURE GUESSWORK!
or Villa Bella
Rio Verde
COLONEL PERCY FAWCETT HAS ALREADY SPENT TWO YEARS MAPPING BOLIVIA AND BRAZIL FOR THE ROYAL GEOGRAPHICAL SOCIETY.
ACCORDING TO THE LOCALS NO ONE'S EVER BEEN UP THE RIO VERDE.

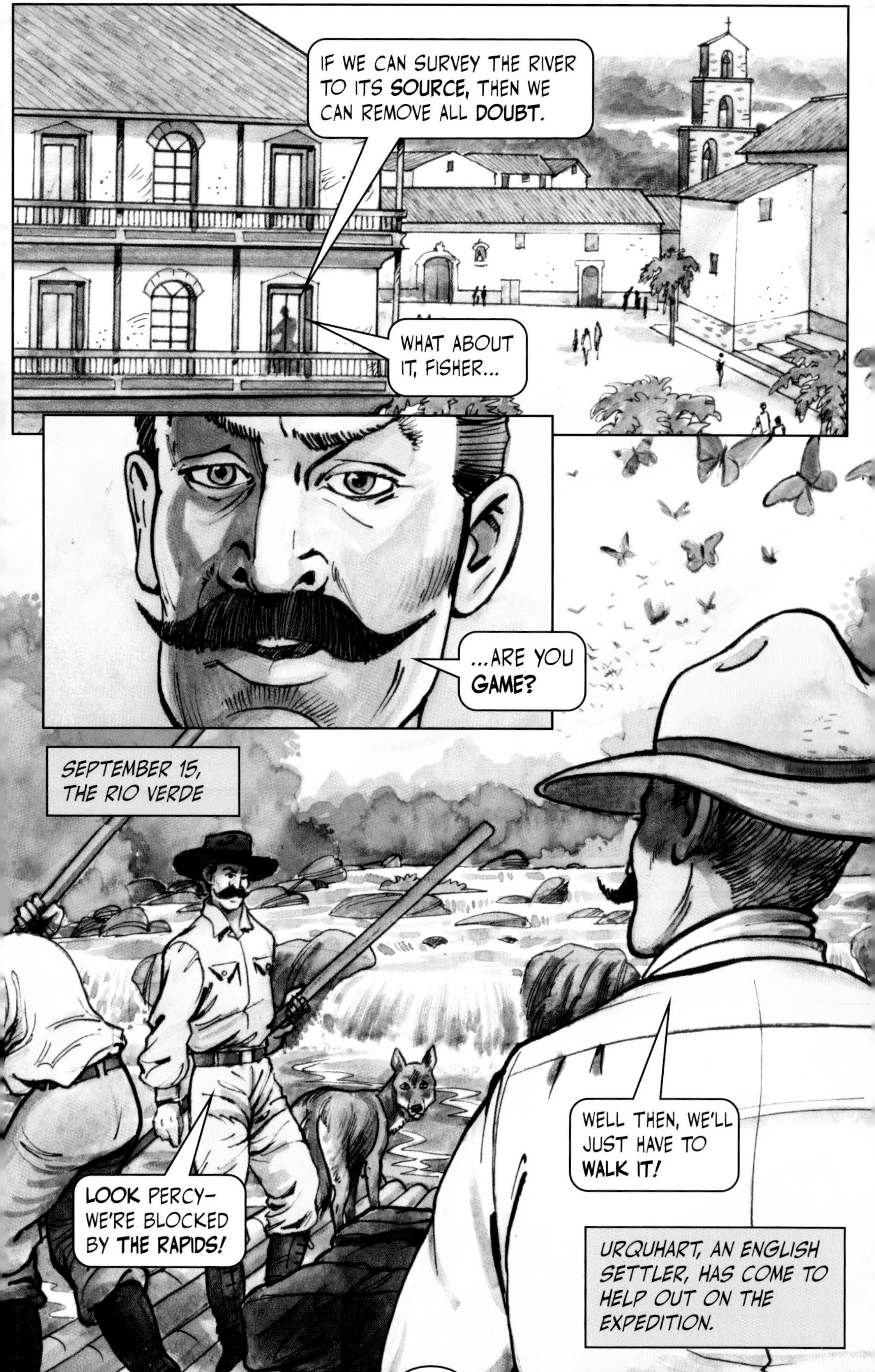
IF WE CAN SURVEY THE RIVER TO ITS SOURCE, THEN WE CAN REMOVE ALL DOUBT.
WHAT ABOUT IT, FISHER...
...ARE YOU GAME?
SEPTEMBER 15, THE RIO VERDE
LOOK PERCY– WE'RE BLOCKED BY THE RAPIDS!
WELL THEN, WE'LL JUST HAVE TO WALK IT!
URQUHART, AN ENGLISH SETTLER, HAS COME TO HELP OUT ON THE EXPEDITION.

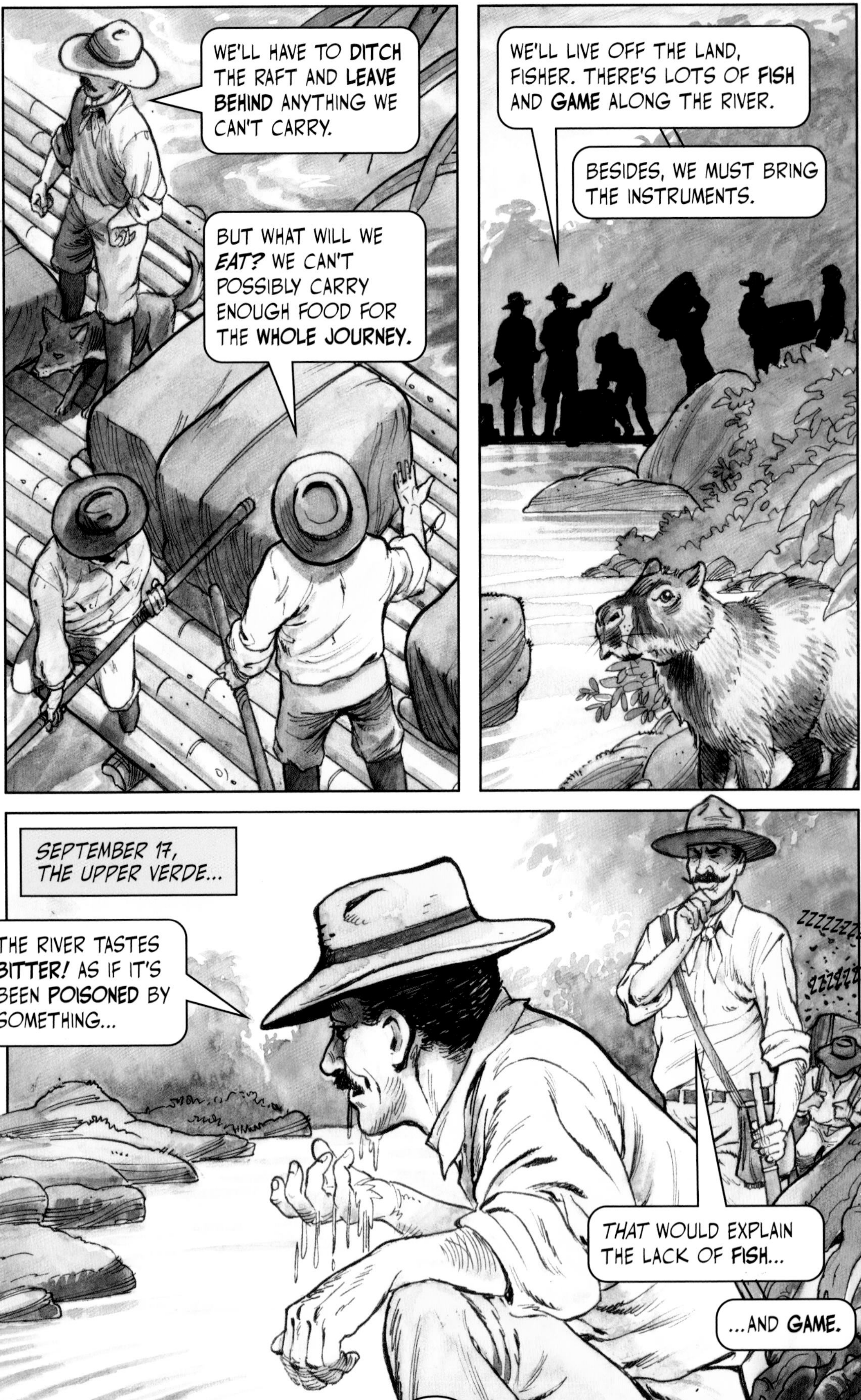
WE'LL HAVE TO DITCH THE RAFT AND LEAVE BEHIND ANYTHING WE CAN'T CARRY.
BUT WHAT WILL WE EAT? WE CAN'T POSSIBLY CARRY ENOUGH FOOD FOR THE WHOLE JOURNEY.
WE'LL LIVE OFF THE LAND, FISHER. THERE'S LOTS OF FISH AND GAME ALONG THE RIVER.
BESIDES, WE MUST BRING THE INSTRUMENTS.
SEPTEMBER 17, THE UPPER VERDE...
THE RIVER TASTES BITTER! AS IF IT'S BEEN POISONED BY SOMETHING...
ZZZZZZZZ
ZZZZZZZ
THAT WOULD EXPLAIN THE LACK OF FISH...
...AND GAME.

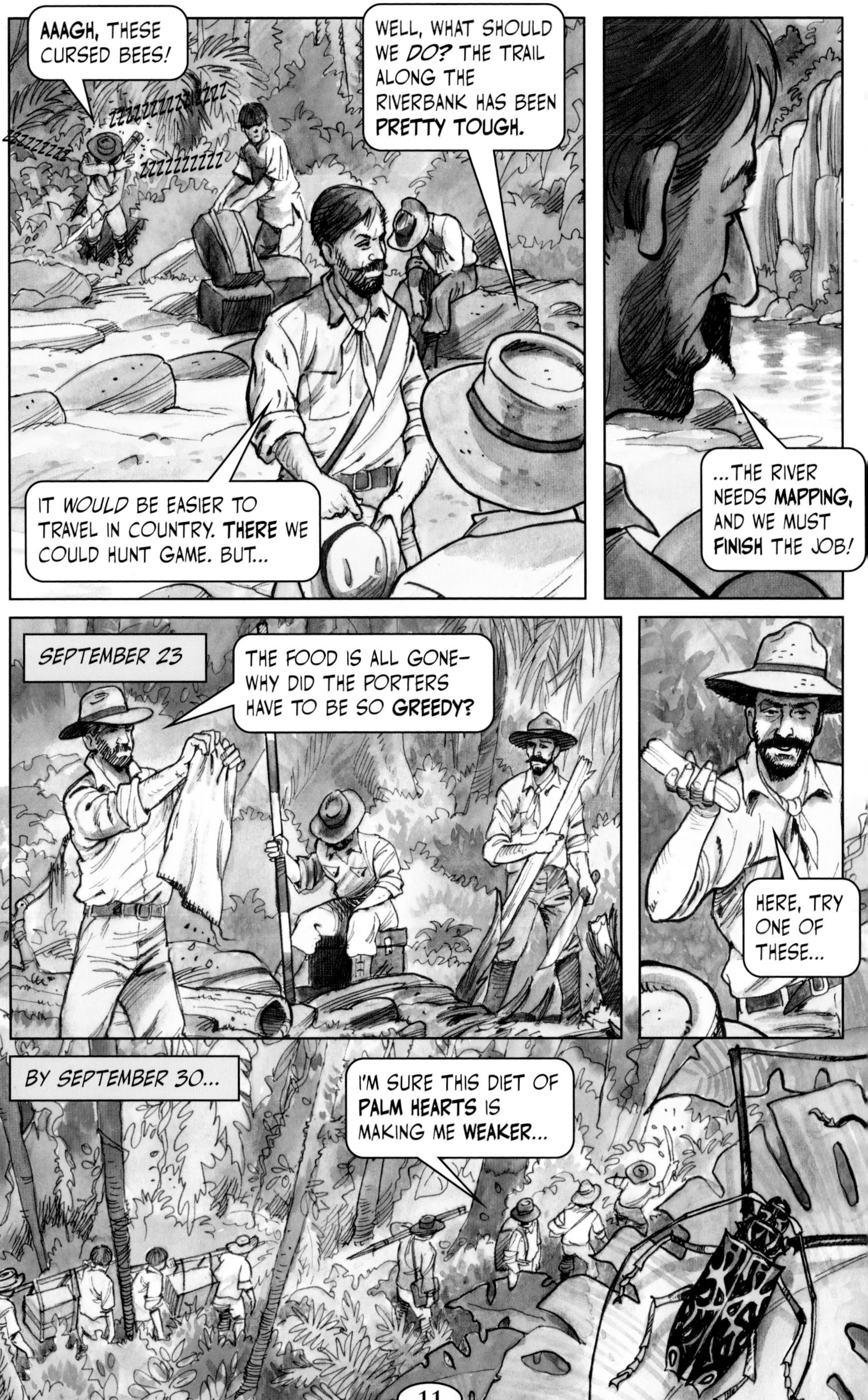
AAAGH, THESE CURSED BEES!
ZZZZZZZZZZZZZZZZ
WELL, WHAT SHOULD WE DO? THE TRAIL ALONG THE RIVERBANK HAS BEEN PRETTY TOUGH.
IT WOULD BE EASIER TO TRAVEL IN COUNTRY. THERE WE COULD HUNT GAME. BUT...
...THE RIVER NEEDS MAPPING, AND WE MUST FINISH THE JOB!
SEPTEMBER 23
THE FOOD IS ALL GONE- WHY DID THE PORTERS HAVE TO BE SO GREEDY?
HERE, TRY ONE OF THESE...
BY SEPTEMBER 30...
I'M SURE THIS DIET OF PALM HEARTS IS MAKING ME WEAKER...

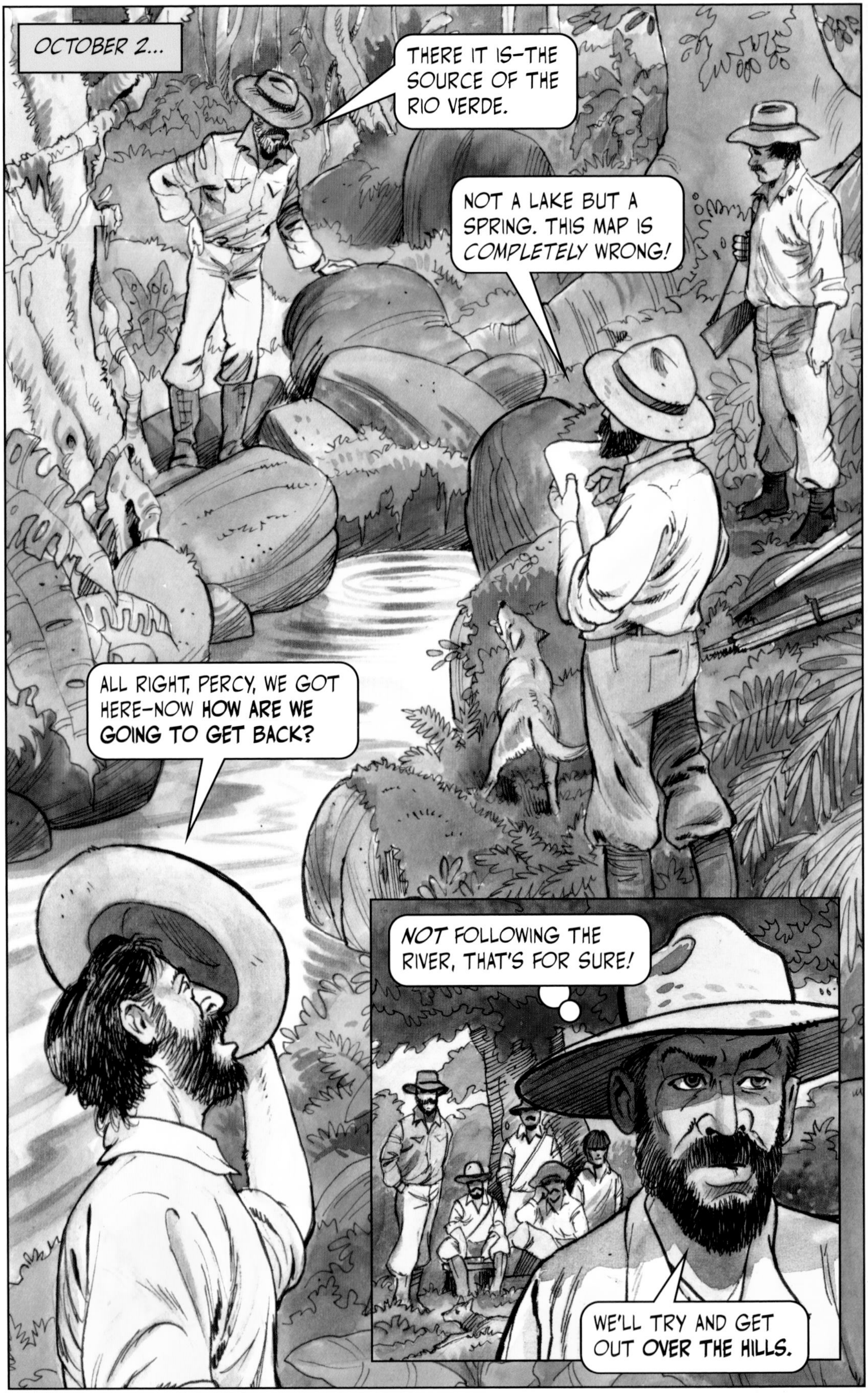
OCTOBER 2...
THERE IT IS–THE SOURCE OF THE RIO VERDE.
NOT A LAKE BUT A SPRING. THIS MAP IS *COMPLETELY* WRONG!
ALL RIGHT, PERCY, WE GOT HERE–NOW **HOW ARE WE GOING TO GET BACK?**
NOT FOLLOWING THE RIVER, THAT'S FOR SURE!
WE'LL TRY AND GET OUT **OVER THE HILLS.**

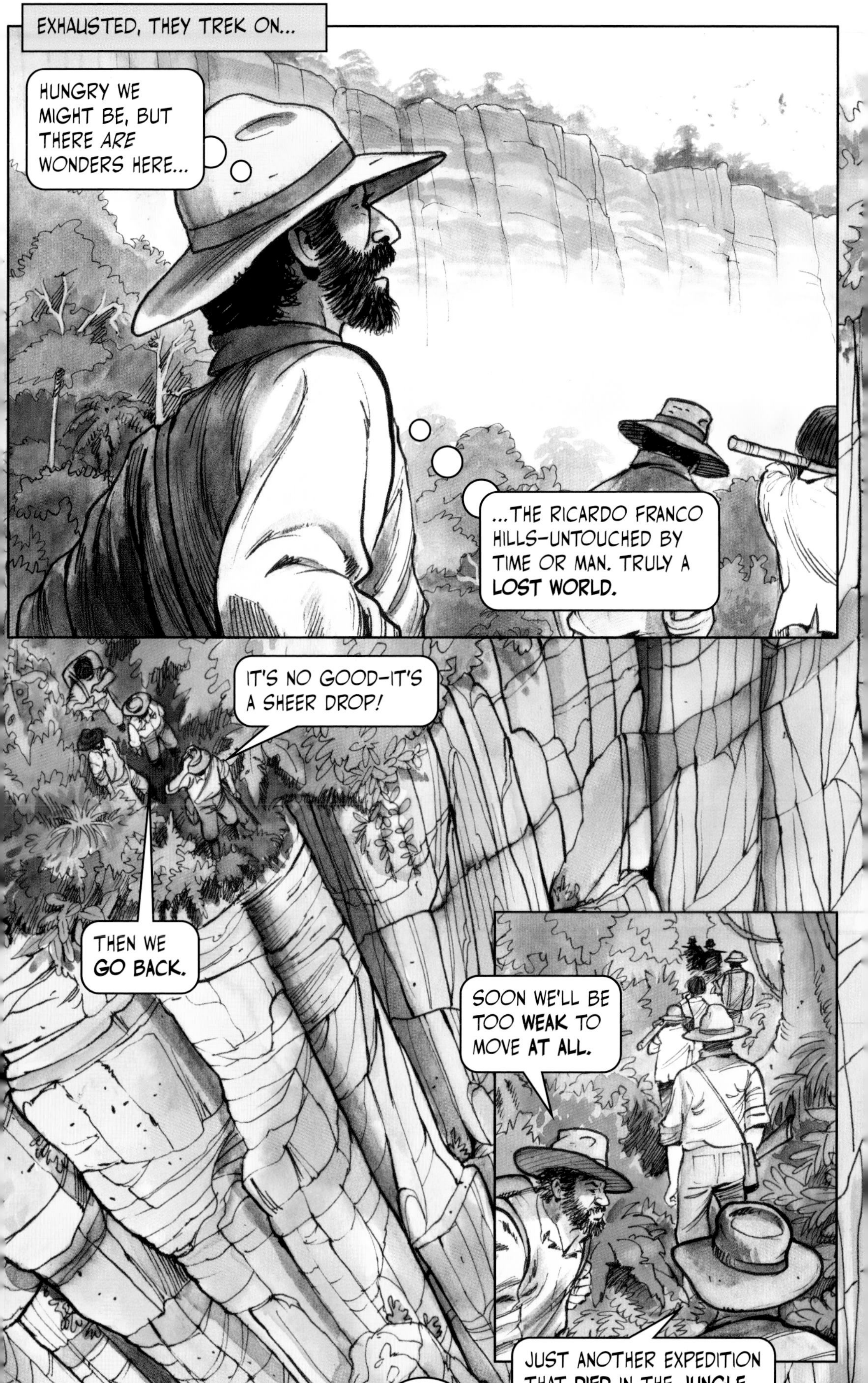
EXHAUSTED, THEY TREK ON...
HUNGRY WE MIGHT BE, BUT THERE ARE WONDERS HERE...
...THE RICARDO FRANCO HILLS–UNTOUCHED BY TIME OR MAN. TRULY A **LOST WORLD.**
IT'S NO GOOD–IT'S A SHEER DROP!
THEN WE **GO BACK.**
SOON WE'LL BE TOO **WEAK** TO MOVE **AT ALL.**
JUST ANOTHER EXPEDITION THAT **DIED** IN THE **JUNGLE.**

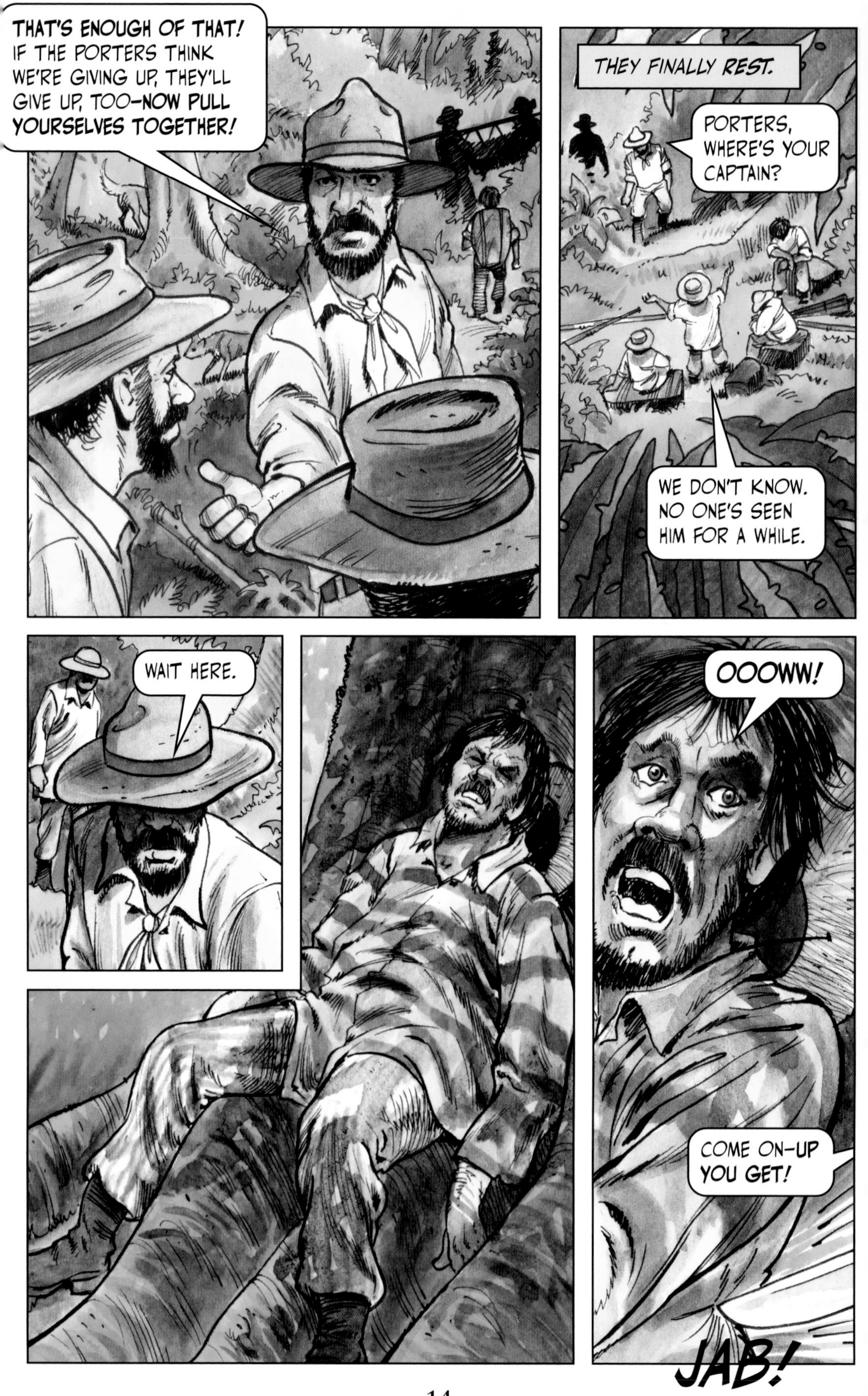
THAT'S ENOUGH OF THAT! IF THE PORTERS THINK WE'RE GIVING UP, THEY'LL GIVE UP, TOO—NOW PULL YOURSELVES TOGETHER!
THEY FINALLY REST.
PORTERS, WHERE'S YOUR CAPTAIN?
WE DON'T KNOW. NO ONE'S SEEN HIM FOR A WHILE.
WAIT HERE.
OOOWW!
COME ON—UP YOU GET!
JAB!

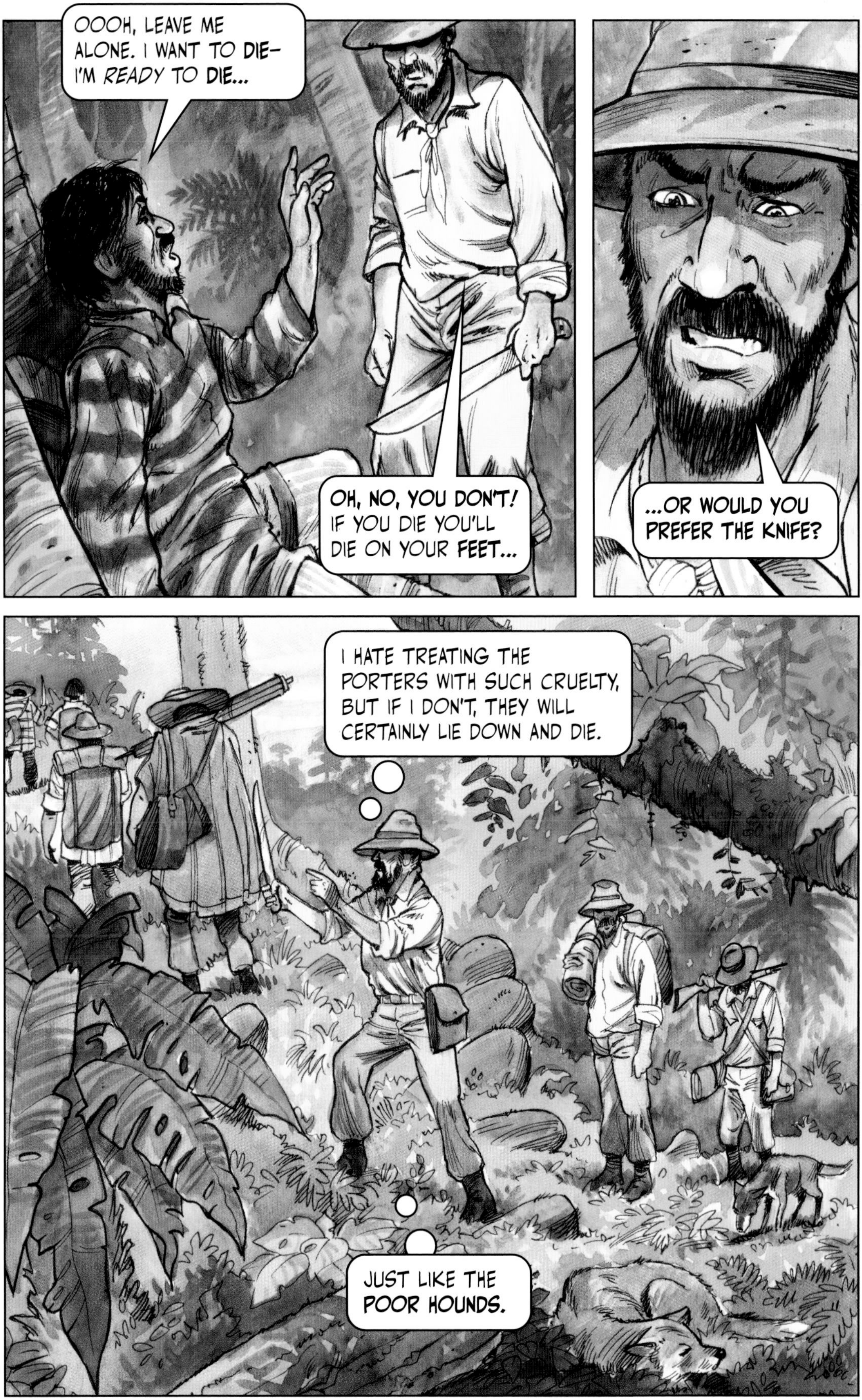
OOOH, LEAVE ME ALONE. I WANT TO DIE– I'M *READY* TO **DIE...**
OH, NO, YOU DON'T! IF YOU DIE YOU'LL DIE ON YOUR **FEET...**
...OR WOULD YOU PREFER THE KNIFE?
I HATE TREATING THE PORTERS WITH SUCH CRUELTY, BUT IF I DON'T, THEY WILL CERTAINLY LIE DOWN AND DIE.
JUST LIKE THE **POOR HOUNDS.**

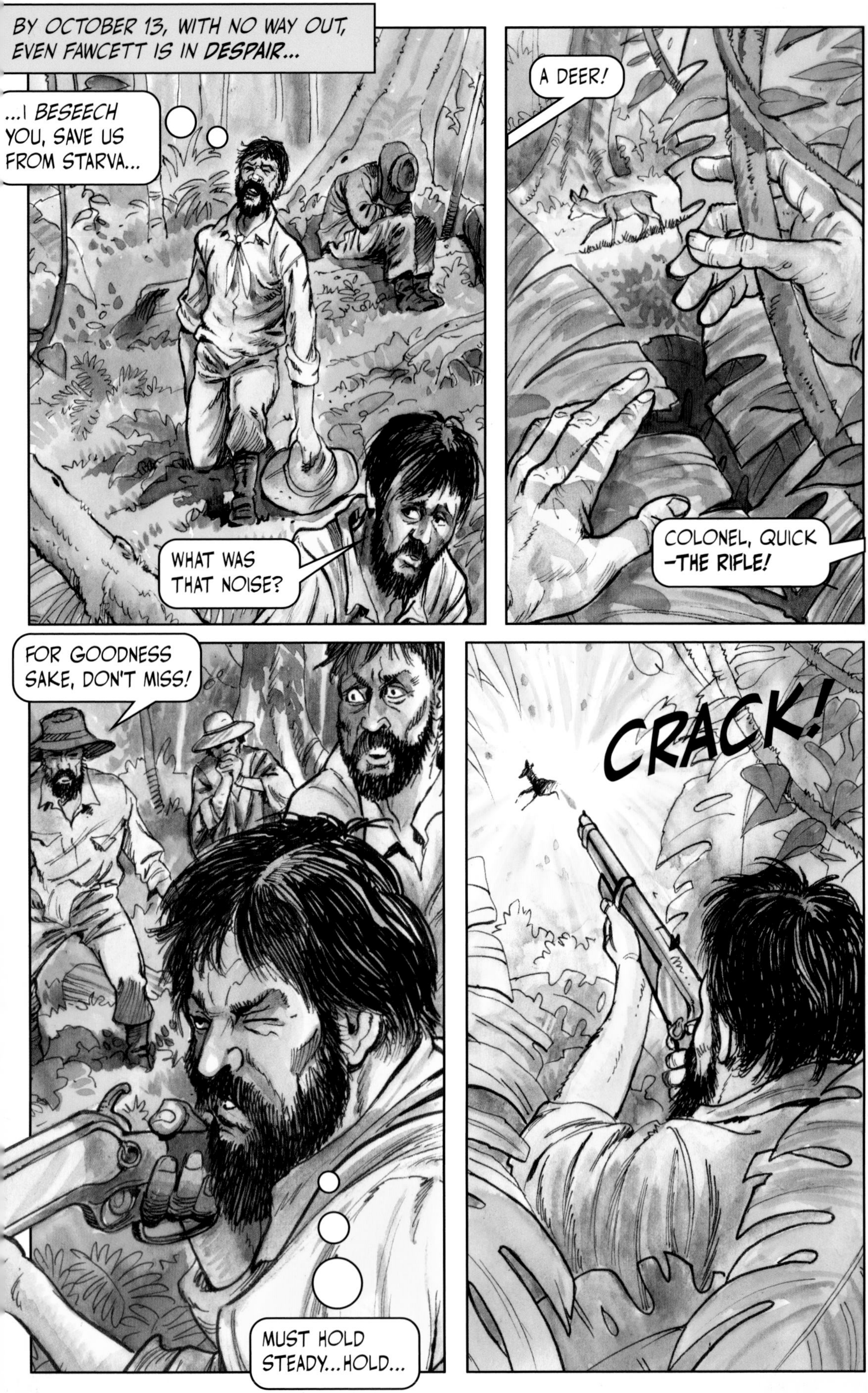
BY OCTOBER 13, WITH NO WAY OUT, EVEN FAWCETT IS IN DESPAIR...
...I BESEECH YOU, SAVE US FROM STARVA...
WHAT WAS THAT NOISE?
A DEER!
COLONEL, QUICK —THE RIFLE!
FOR GOODNESS SAKE, DON'T MISS!
MUST HOLD STEADY...HOLD...
CRACK!

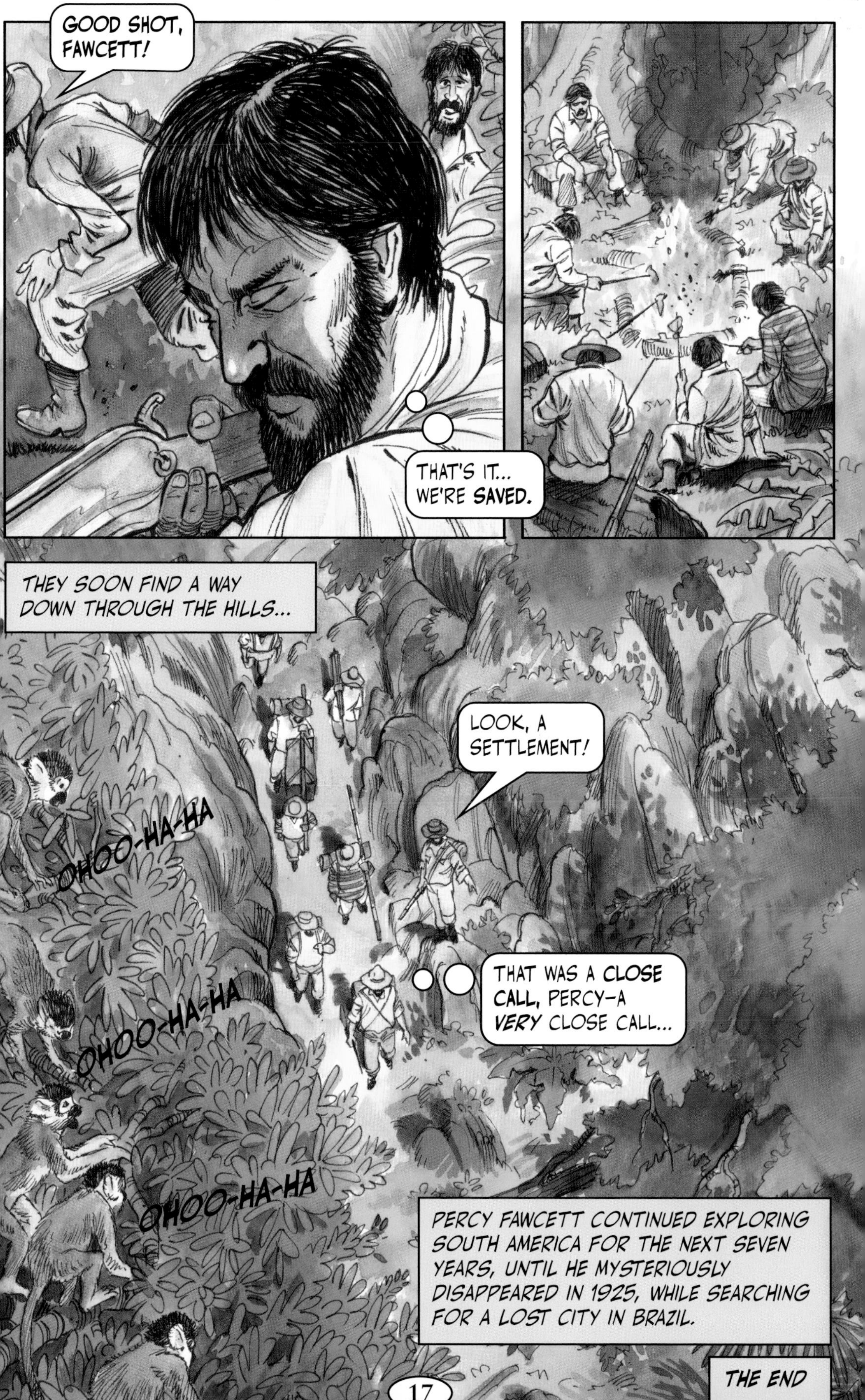
GOOD SHOT, FAWCETT!
THAT'S IT... WE'RE **SAVED.**
THEY SOON FIND A WAY DOWN THROUGH THE HILLS...
LOOK, A SETTLEMENT!
OHOO-HA-HA
THAT WAS A **CLOSE CALL,** PERCY—A *VERY* CLOSE CALL...
OHOO-HA-HA
OHOO-HA-HA
PERCY FAWCETT CONTINUED EXPLORING SOUTH AMERICA FOR THE NEXT SEVEN YEARS, UNTIL HE MYSTERIOUSLY DISAPPEARED IN 1925, WHILE SEARCHING FOR A LOST CITY IN BRAZIL.
THE END

AGAINST ALL ODDS
U.S. Navy Pilot Dieter Dengler in the Rainforest of Laos, 1966

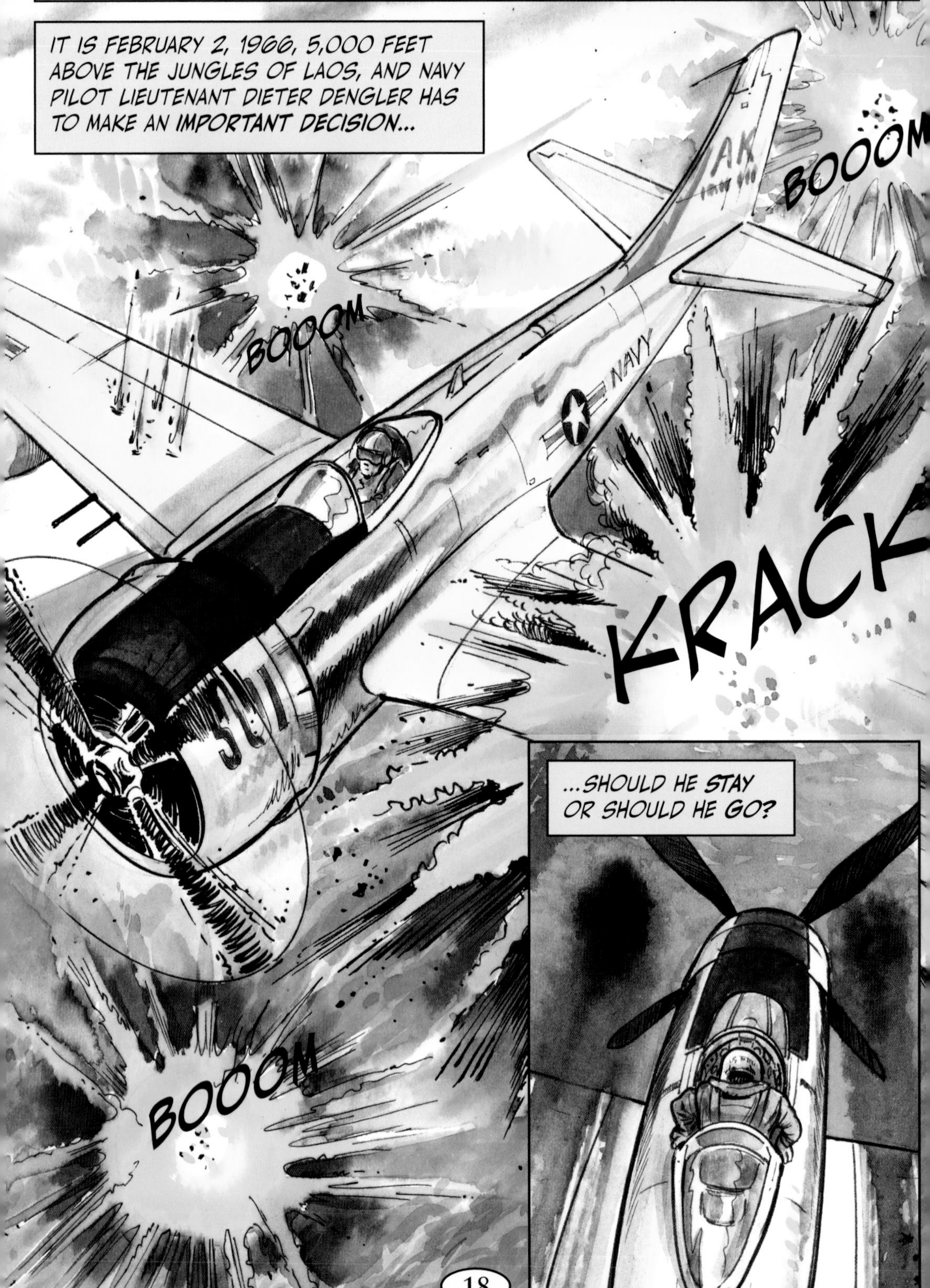
IT IS FEBRUARY 2, 1966, 5,000 FEET ABOVE THE JUNGLES OF LAOS, AND NAVY PILOT LIEUTENANT DIETER DENGLER HAS TO MAKE AN IMPORTANT DECISION...
BOOOM
BOOOM
NAVY
KRACK
BOOOM
...SHOULD HE STAY OR SHOULD HE GO?

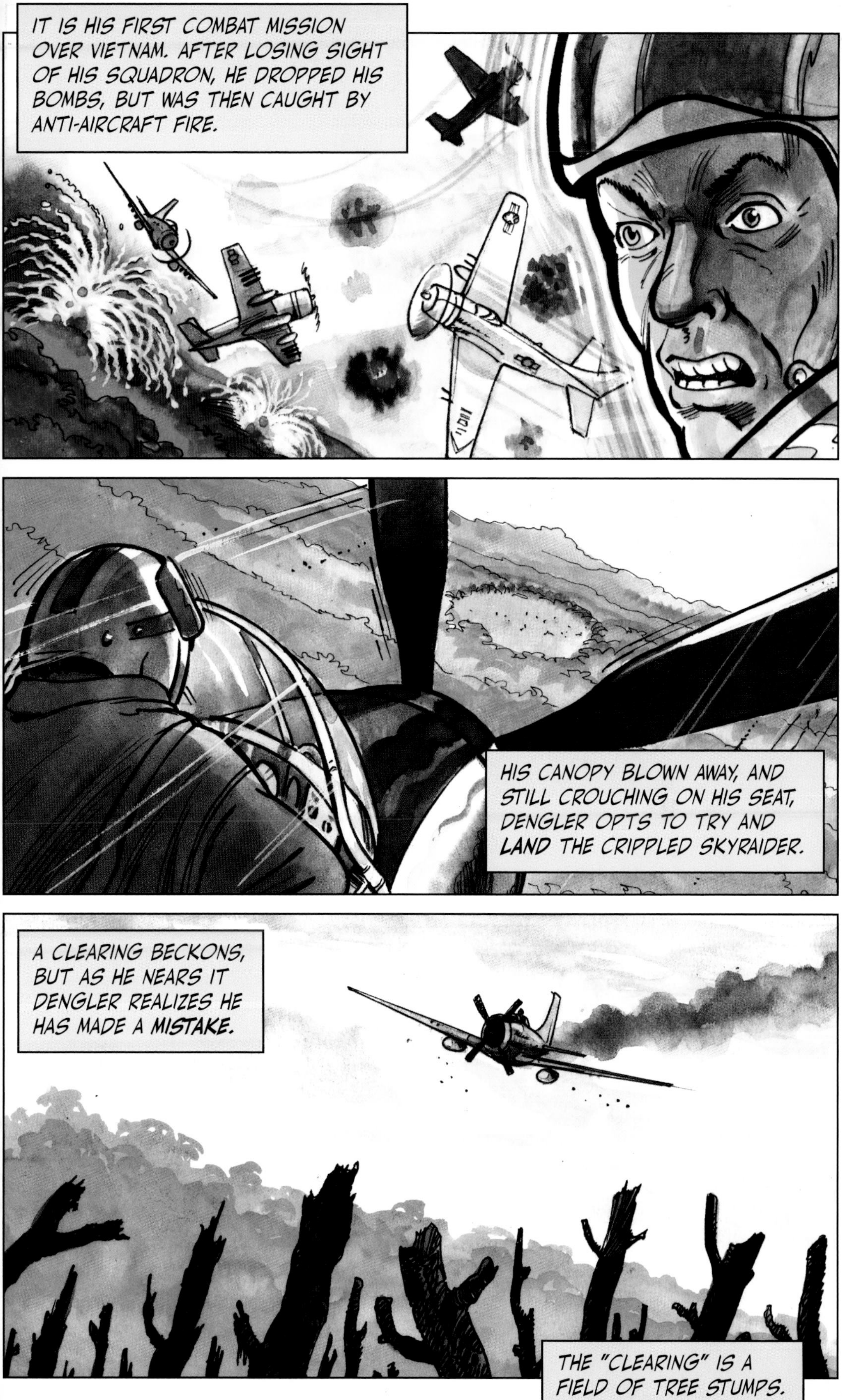
IT IS HIS FIRST COMBAT MISSION OVER VIETNAM. AFTER LOSING SIGHT OF HIS SQUADRON, HE DROPPED HIS BOMBS, BUT WAS THEN CAUGHT BY ANTI-AIRCRAFT FIRE.
HIS CANOPY BLOWN AWAY, AND STILL CROUCHING ON HIS SEAT, DENGLER OPTS TO TRY AND LAND THE CRIPPLED SKYRAIDER.
A CLEARING BECKONS, BUT AS HE NEARS IT DENGLER REALIZES HE HAS MADE A MISTAKE.
THE "CLEARING" IS A FIELD OF TREE STUMPS.

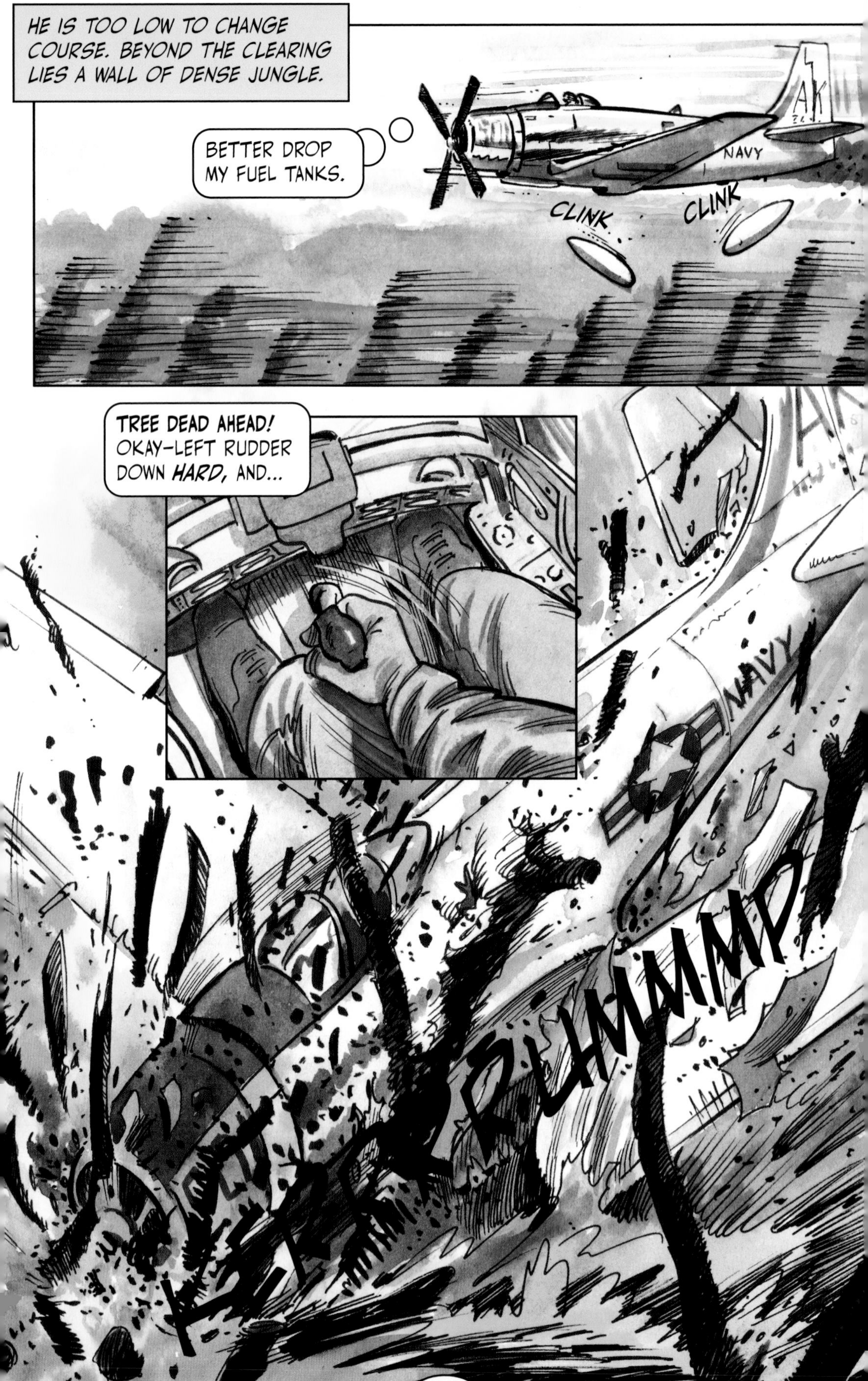
HE IS TOO LOW TO CHANGE COURSE. BEYOND THE CLEARING LIES A WALL OF DENSE JUNGLE.
BETTER DROP MY FUEL TANKS.
CLINK
CLINK
TREE DEAD AHEAD! OKAY–LEFT RUDDER DOWN HARD, AND...
KERRRUMMMP

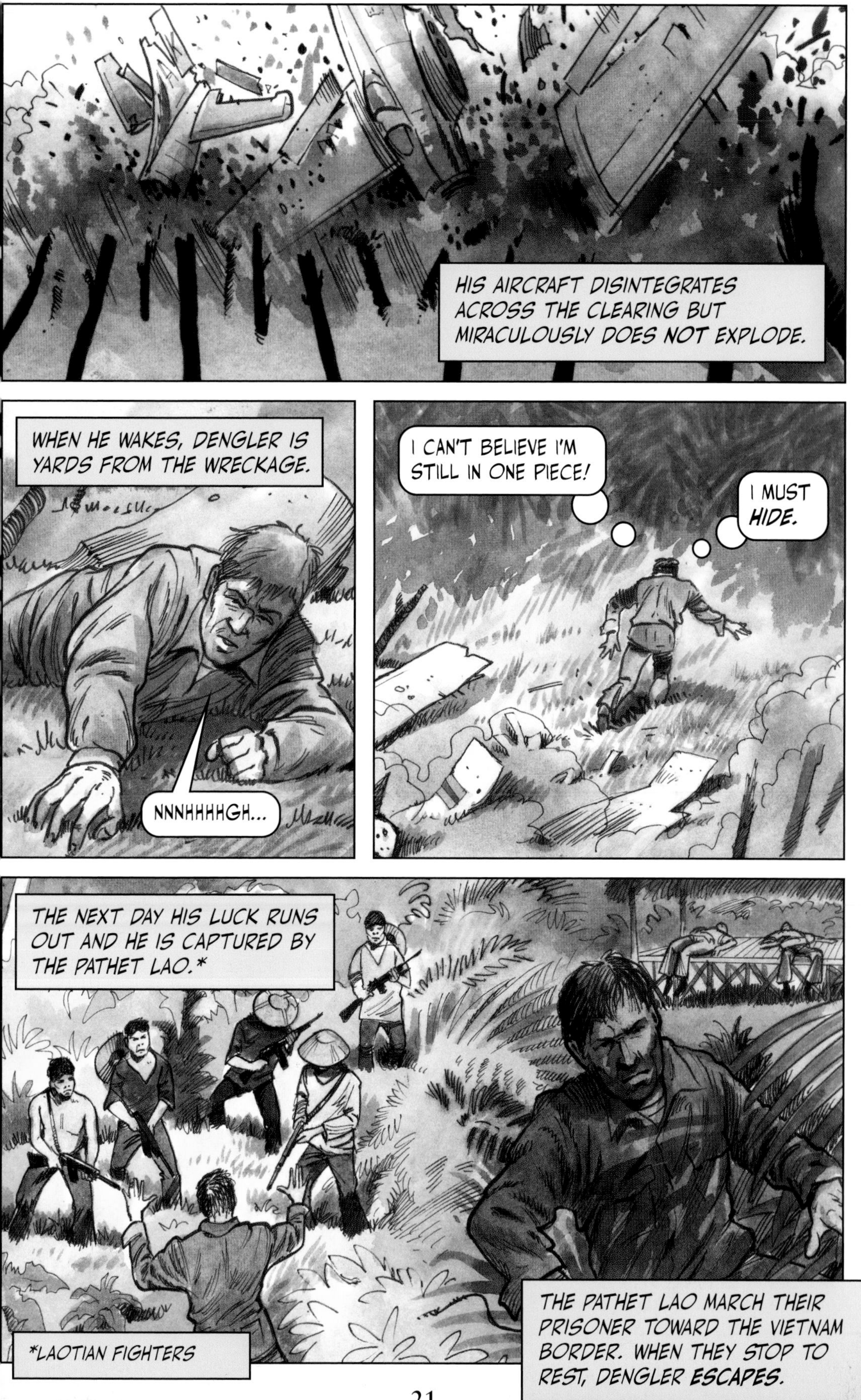
HIS AIRCRAFT DISINTEGRATES ACROSS THE CLEARING BUT MIRACULOUSLY DOES NOT EXPLODE.
WHEN HE WAKES, DENGLER IS YARDS FROM THE WRECKAGE.
NNNHHHHGH...
I CAN'T BELIEVE I'M STILL IN ONE PIECE!
I MUST HIDE.
THE NEXT DAY HIS LUCK RUNS OUT AND HE IS CAPTURED BY THE PATHET LAO.*
*LAOTIAN FIGHTERS
THE PATHET LAO MARCH THEIR PRISONER TOWARD THE VIETNAM BORDER. WHEN THEY STOP TO REST, DENGLER ESCAPES.

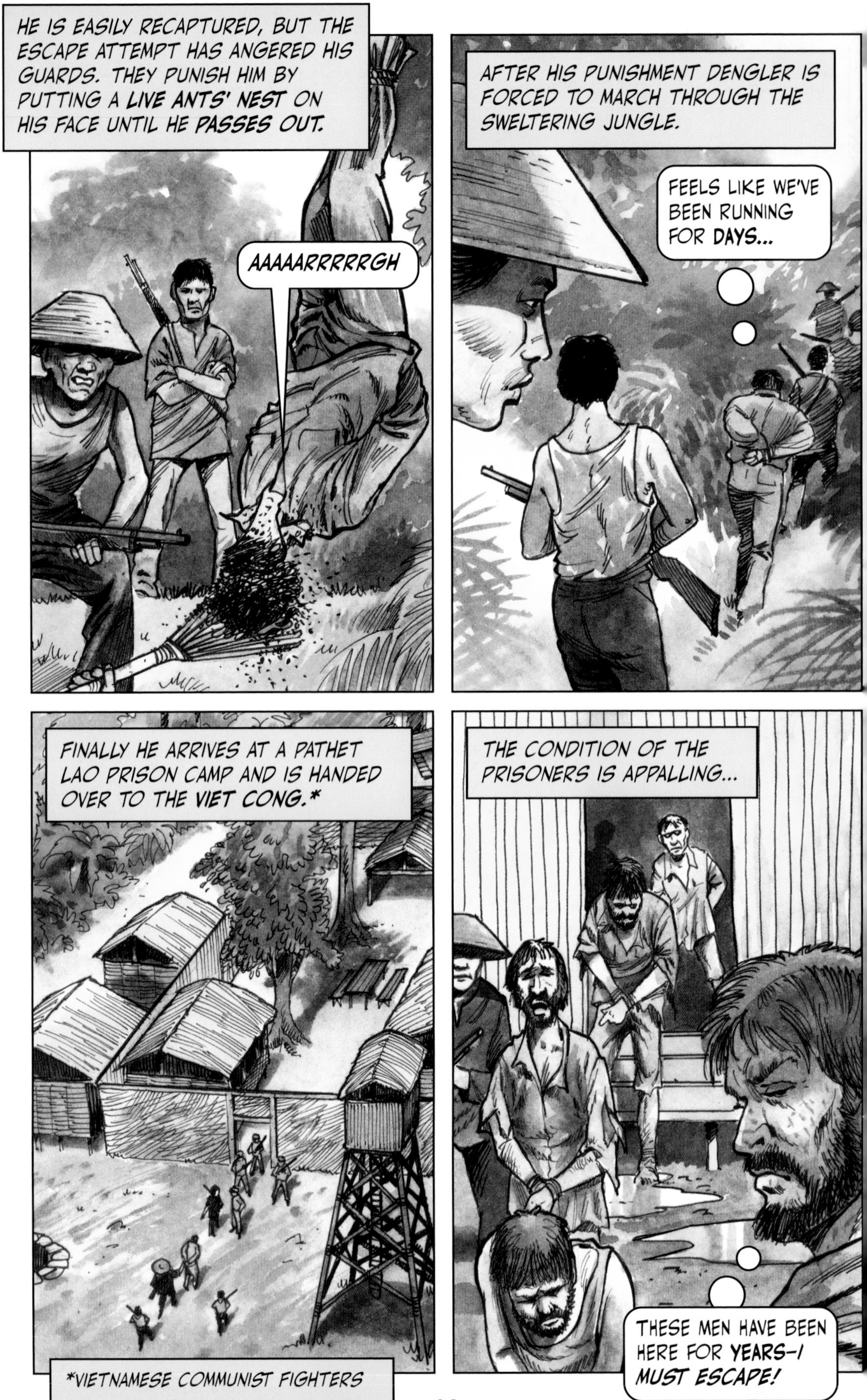
HE IS EASILY RECAPTURED, BUT THE ESCAPE ATTEMPT HAS ANGERED HIS GUARDS. THEY PUNISH HIM BY PUTTING A LIVE ANTS' NEST ON HIS FACE UNTIL HE PASSES OUT.
AAAAARRRRRGH
AFTER HIS PUNISHMENT DENGLER IS FORCED TO MARCH THROUGH THE SWELTERING JUNGLE.
FEELS LIKE WE'VE BEEN RUNNING FOR DAYS...
FINALLY HE ARRIVES AT A PATHET LAO PRISON CAMP AND IS HANDED OVER TO THE VIET CONG.*
*VIETNAMESE COMMUNIST FIGHTERS
THE CONDITION OF THE PRISONERS IS APPALLING...
THESE MEN HAVE BEEN HERE FOR YEARS–I MUST ESCAPE!

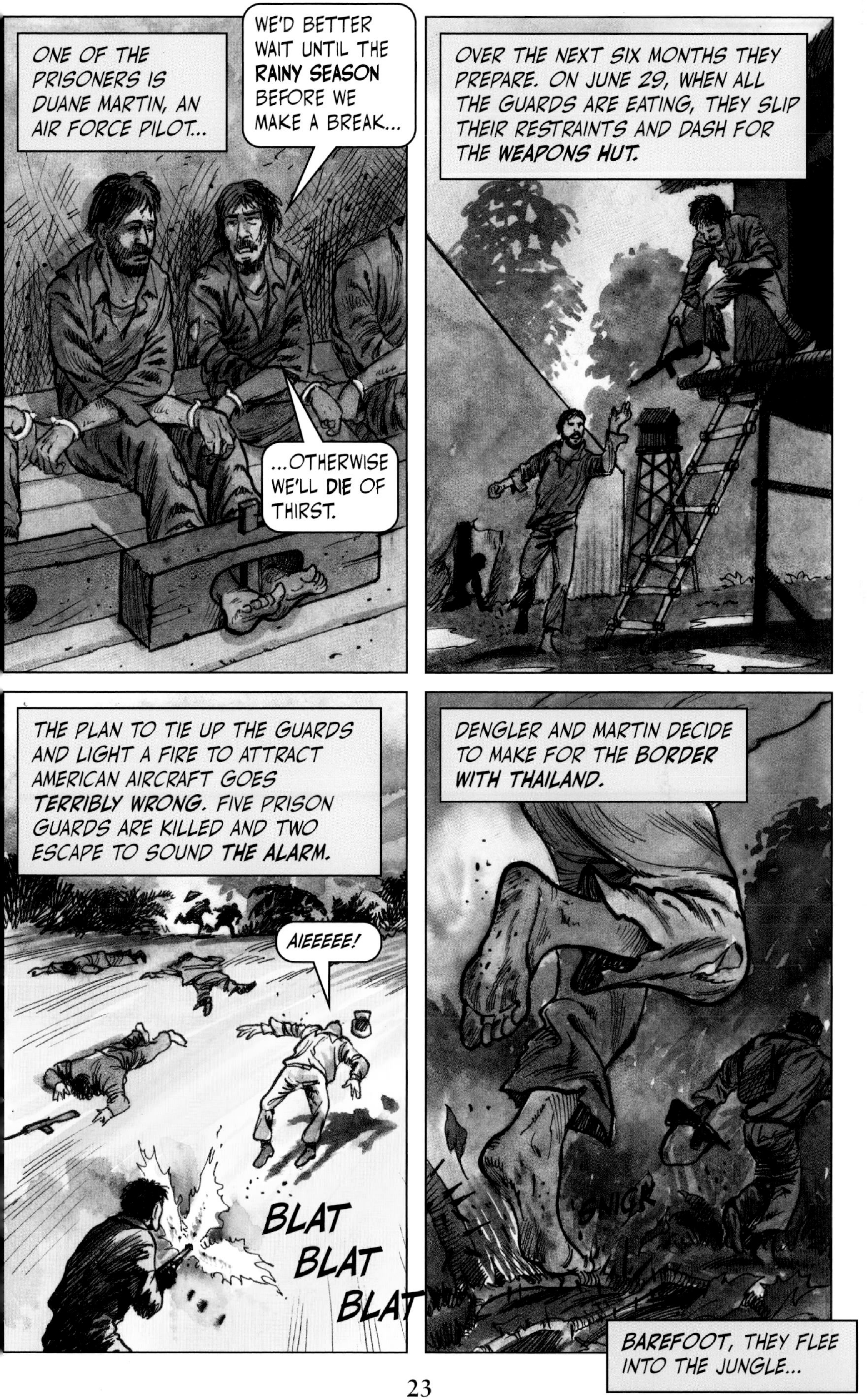
ONE OF THE PRISONERS IS DUANE MARTIN, AN AIR FORCE PILOT...
WE'D BETTER WAIT UNTIL THE RAINY SEASON BEFORE WE MAKE A BREAK...
...OTHERWISE WE'LL DIE OF THIRST.
OVER THE NEXT SIX MONTHS THEY PREPARE. ON JUNE 29, WHEN ALL THE GUARDS ARE EATING, THEY SLIP THEIR RESTRAINTS AND DASH FOR THE WEAPONS HUT.
THE PLAN TO TIE UP THE GUARDS AND LIGHT A FIRE TO ATTRACT AMERICAN AIRCRAFT GOES TERRIBLY WRONG. FIVE PRISON GUARDS ARE KILLED AND TWO ESCAPE TO SOUND THE ALARM.
AIEEEEE!
BLAT
BLAT
BLAT
DENGLER AND MARTIN DECIDE TO MAKE FOR THE BORDER WITH THAILAND.
SNICK
BAREFOOT, THEY FLEE INTO THE JUNGLE...

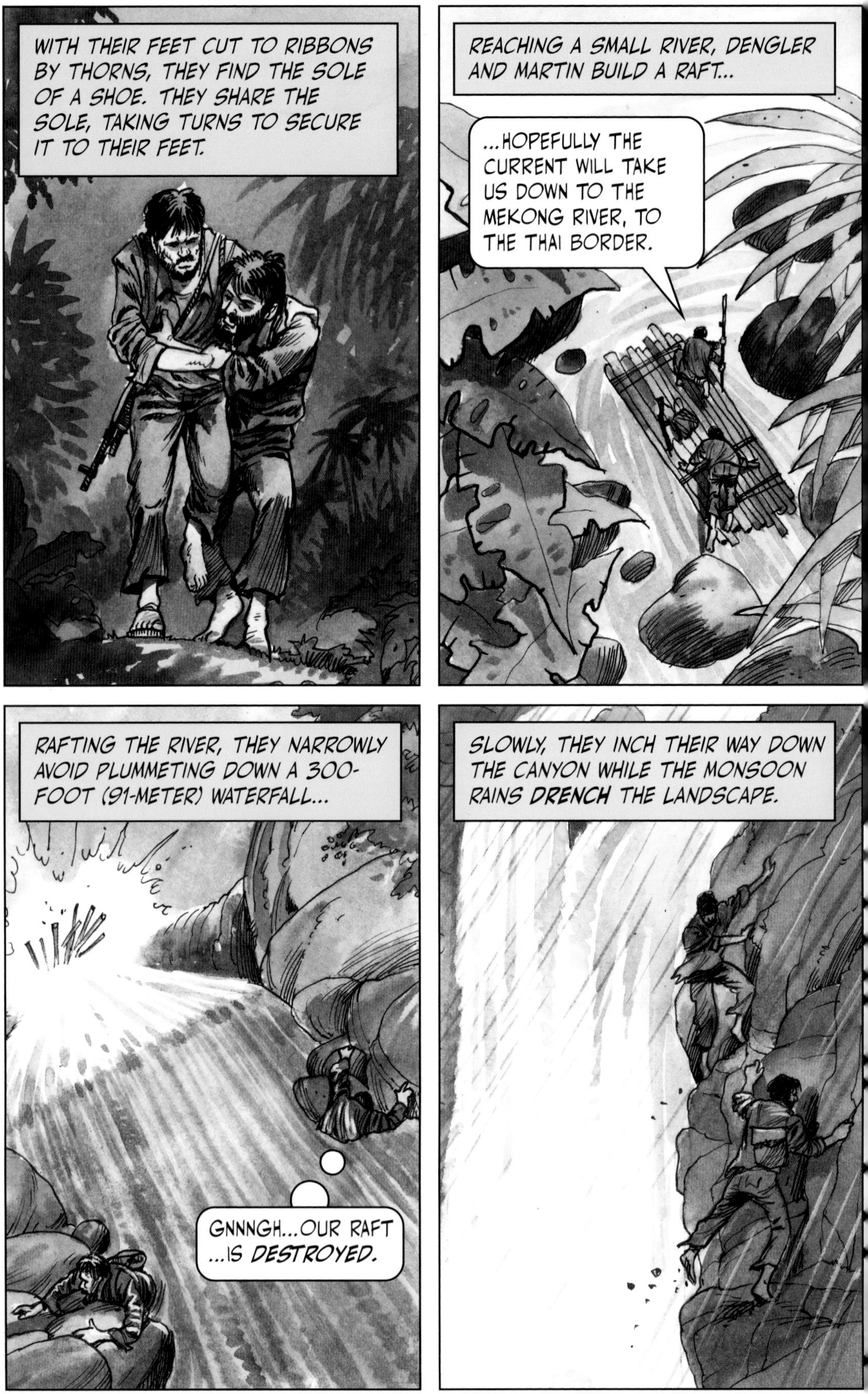
WITH THEIR FEET CUT TO RIBBONS BY THORNS, THEY FIND THE SOLE OF A SHOE. THEY SHARE THE SOLE, TAKING TURNS TO SECURE IT TO THEIR FEET.
REACHING A SMALL RIVER, DENGLER AND MARTIN BUILD A RAFT...
...HOPEFULLY THE CURRENT WILL TAKE US DOWN TO THE MEKONG RIVER, TO THE THAI BORDER.
RAFTING THE RIVER, THEY NARROWLY AVOID PLUMMETING DOWN A 300-FOOT (91-METER) WATERFALL...
GNNNGH...OUR RAFT ...IS *DESTROYED.*
SLOWLY, THEY INCH THEIR WAY DOWN THE CANYON WHILE THE MONSOON RAINS **DRENCH** THE LANDSCAPE.

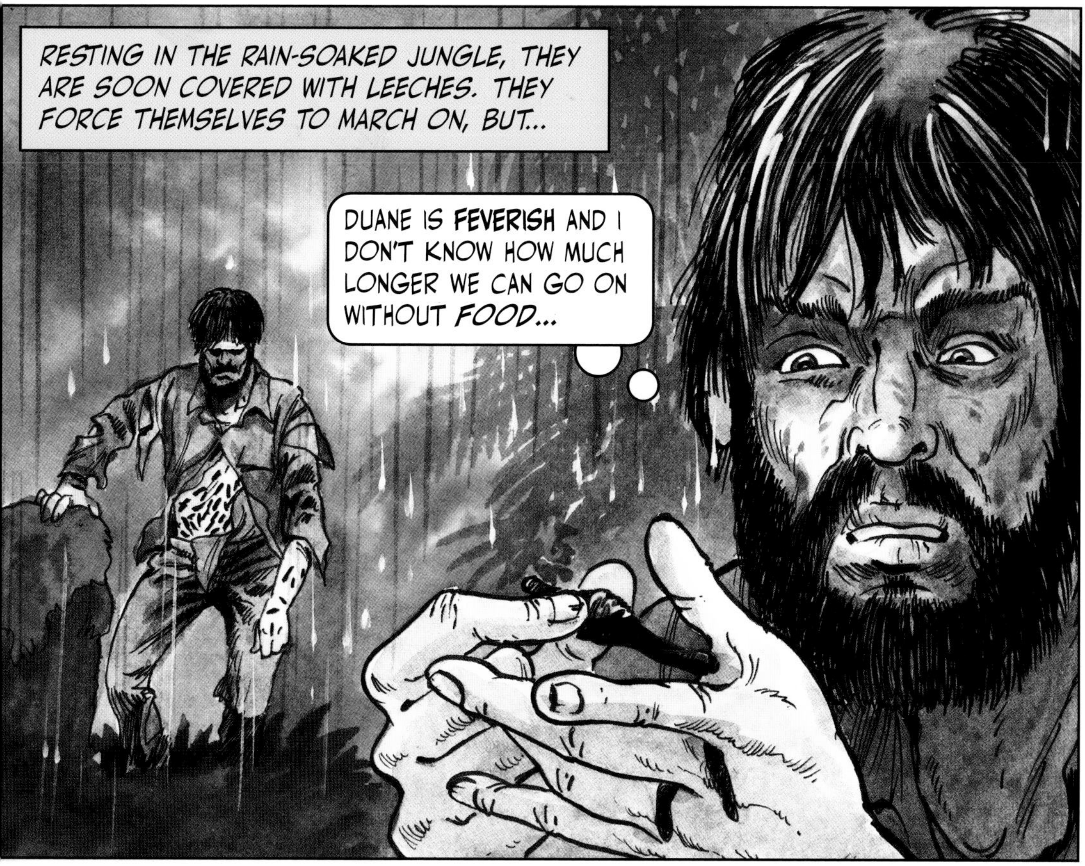
RESTING IN THE RAIN-SOAKED JUNGLE, THEY ARE SOON COVERED WITH LEECHES. THEY FORCE THEMSELVES TO MARCH ON, BUT...
DUANE IS FEVERISH AND I DON'T KNOW HOW MUCH LONGER WE CAN GO ON WITHOUT FOOD...

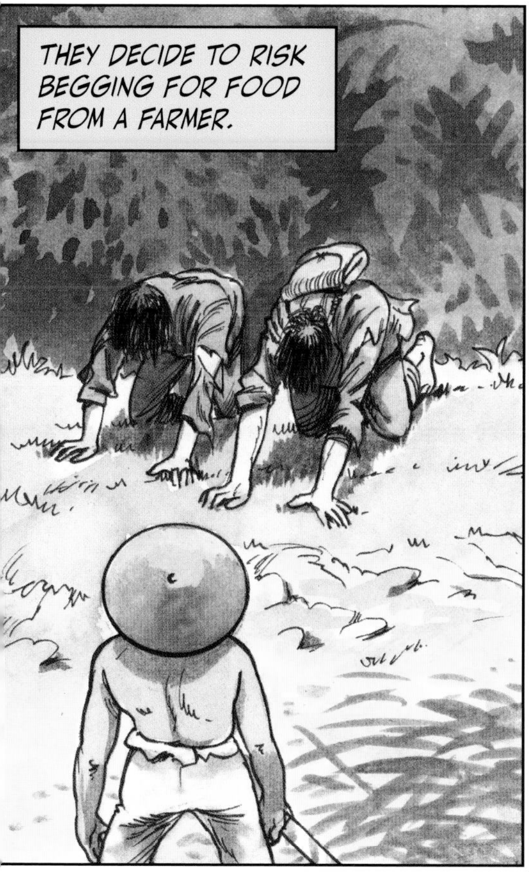
THEY DECIDE TO RISK BEGGING FOR FOOD FROM A FARMER.

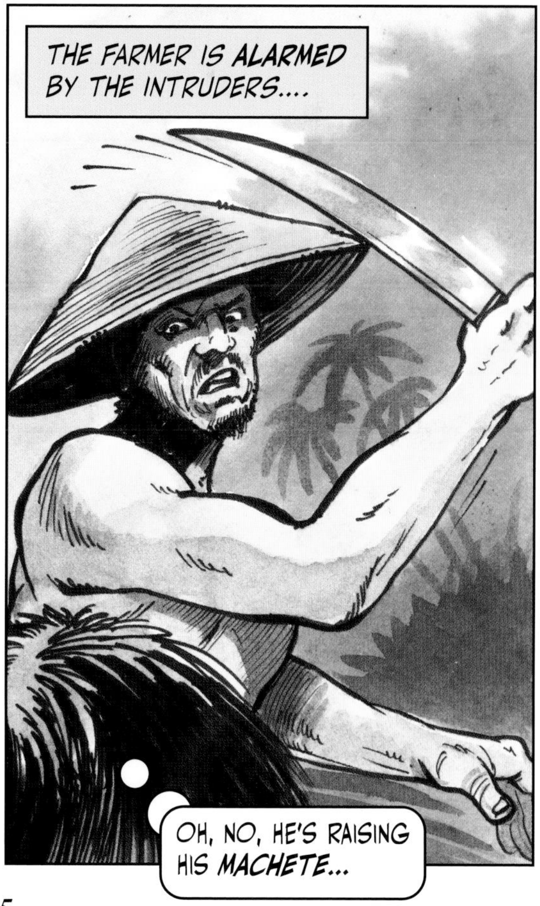
THE FARMER IS ALARMED BY THE INTRUDERS....
OH, NO, HE'S RAISING HIS MACHETE...

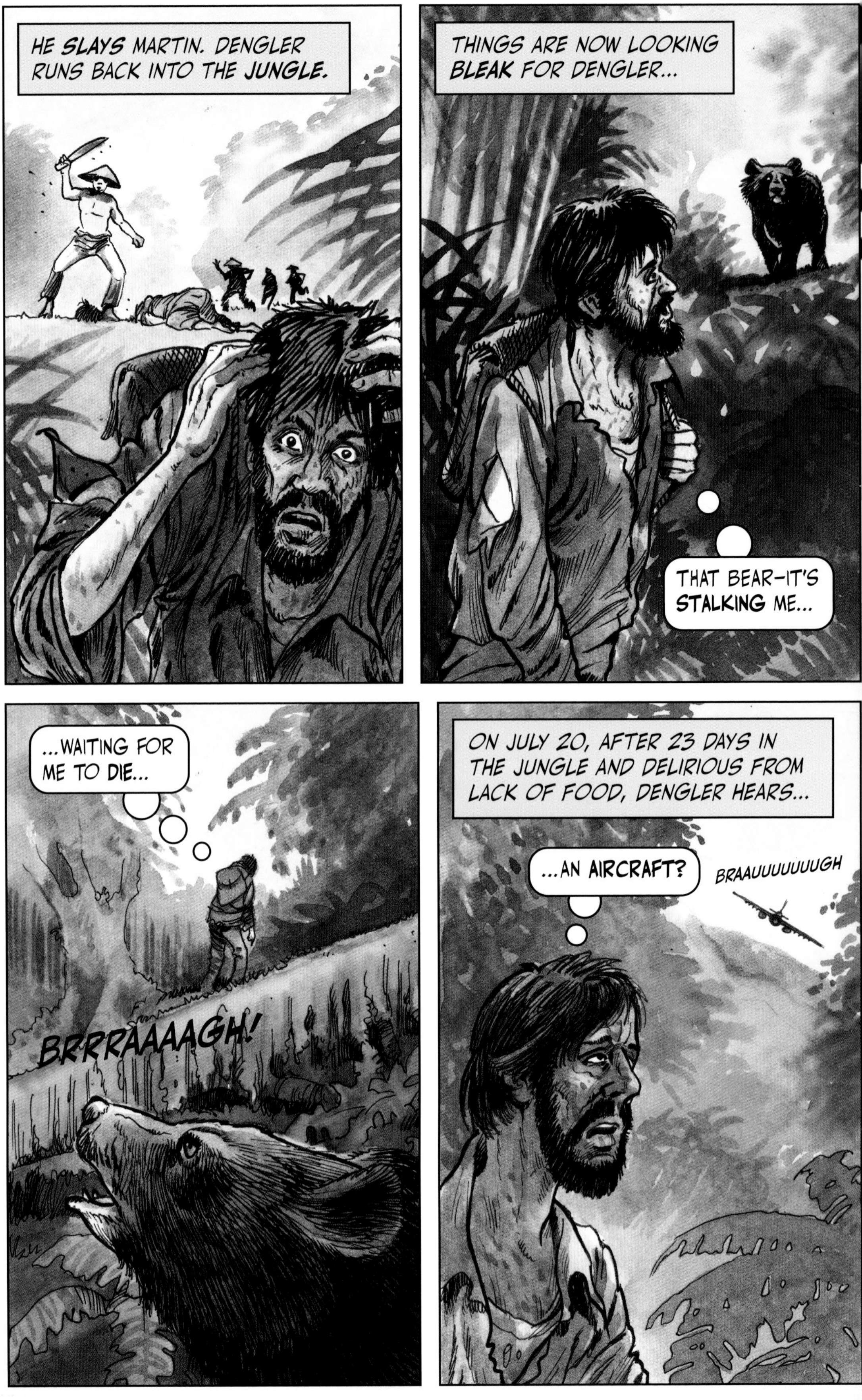
HE SLAYS MARTIN. DENGLER RUNS BACK INTO THE JUNGLE.
THINGS ARE NOW LOOKING BLEAK FOR DENGLER...
THAT BEAR—IT'S STALKING ME...
...WAITING FOR ME TO DIE...
BRRRAAAAGH!
ON JULY 20, AFTER 23 DAYS IN THE JUNGLE AND DELIRIOUS FROM LACK OF FOOD, DENGLER HEARS...
...AN AIRCRAFT?
BRAAUUUUUUUGH

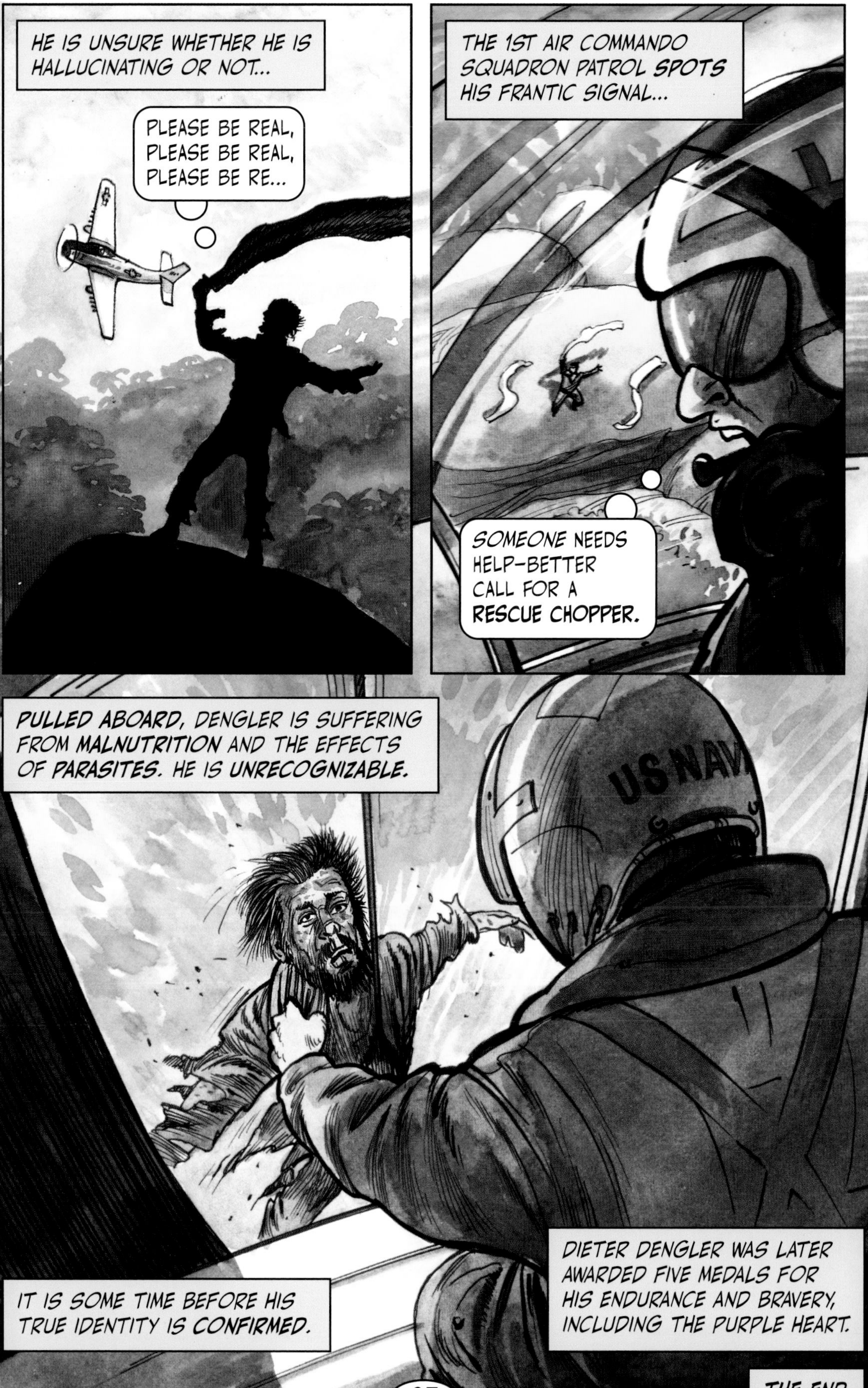
HE IS UNSURE WHETHER HE IS HALLUCINATING OR NOT...
PLEASE BE REAL, PLEASE BE REAL, PLEASE BE RE...
THE 1ST AIR COMMANDO SQUADRON PATROL SPOTS HIS FRANTIC SIGNAL...
SOMEONE NEEDS HELP—BETTER CALL FOR A RESCUE CHOPPER.
PULLED ABOARD, DENGLER IS SUFFERING FROM MALNUTRITION AND THE EFFECTS OF PARASITES. HE IS UNRECOGNIZABLE.
US NAV
IT IS SOME TIME BEFORE HIS TRUE IDENTITY IS CONFIRMED.
DIETER DENGLER WAS LATER AWARDED FIVE MEDALS FOR HIS ENDURANCE AND BRAVERY, INCLUDING THE PURPLE HEART.
THE END

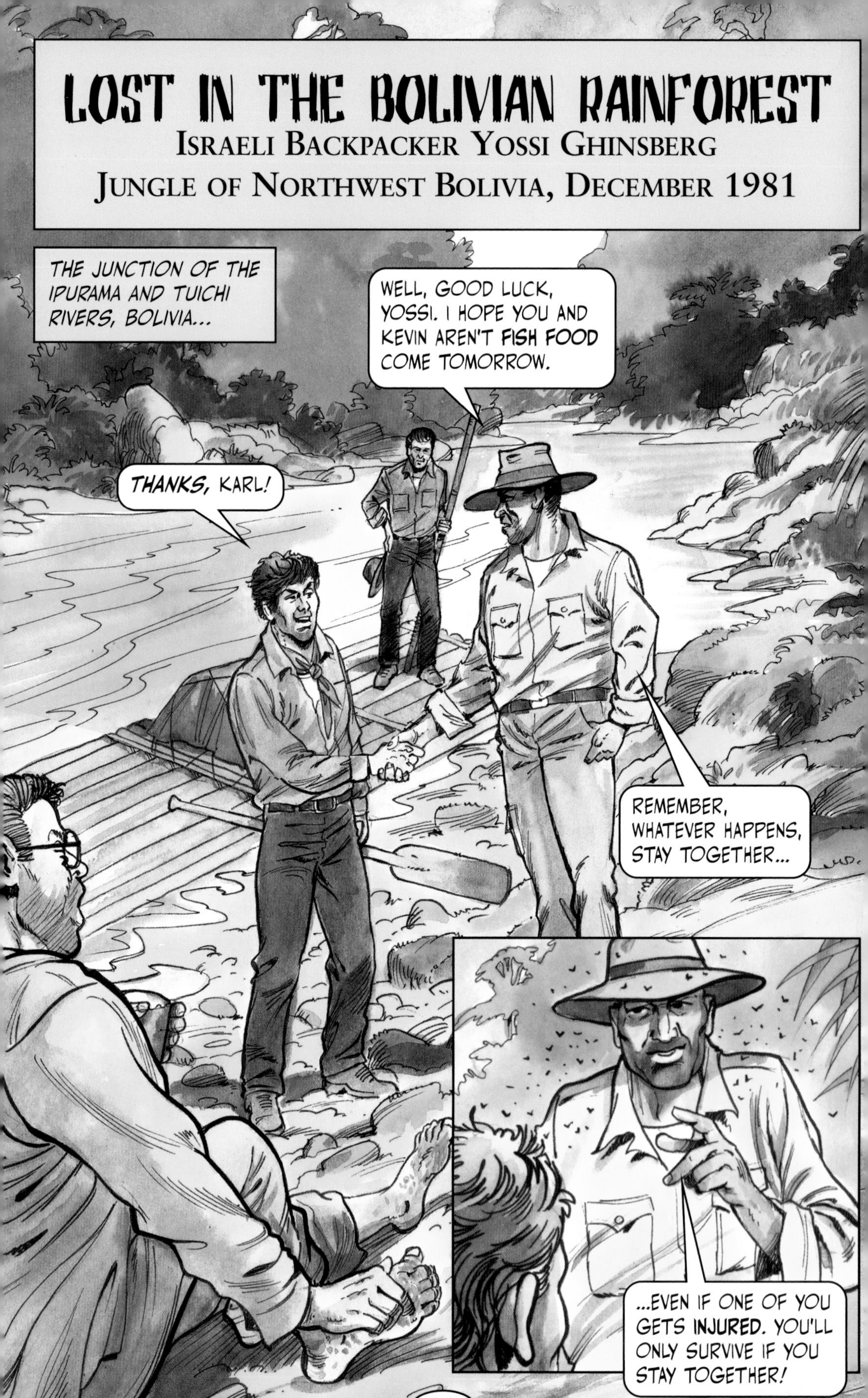
LOST IN THE BOLIVIAN RAINFOREST
ISRAELI BACKPACKER YOSSI GHINSBERG
JUNGLE OF NORTHWEST BOLIVIA, DECEMBER 1981
THE JUNCTION OF THE IPURAMA AND TUICHI RIVERS, BOLIVIA...
WELL, GOOD LUCK, YOSSI. I HOPE YOU AND KEVIN AREN'T FISH FOOD COME TOMORROW.
THANKS, KARL!
REMEMBER, WHATEVER HAPPENS, STAY TOGETHER...
...EVEN IF ONE OF YOU GETS INJURED. YOU'LL ONLY SURVIVE IF YOU STAY TOGETHER!

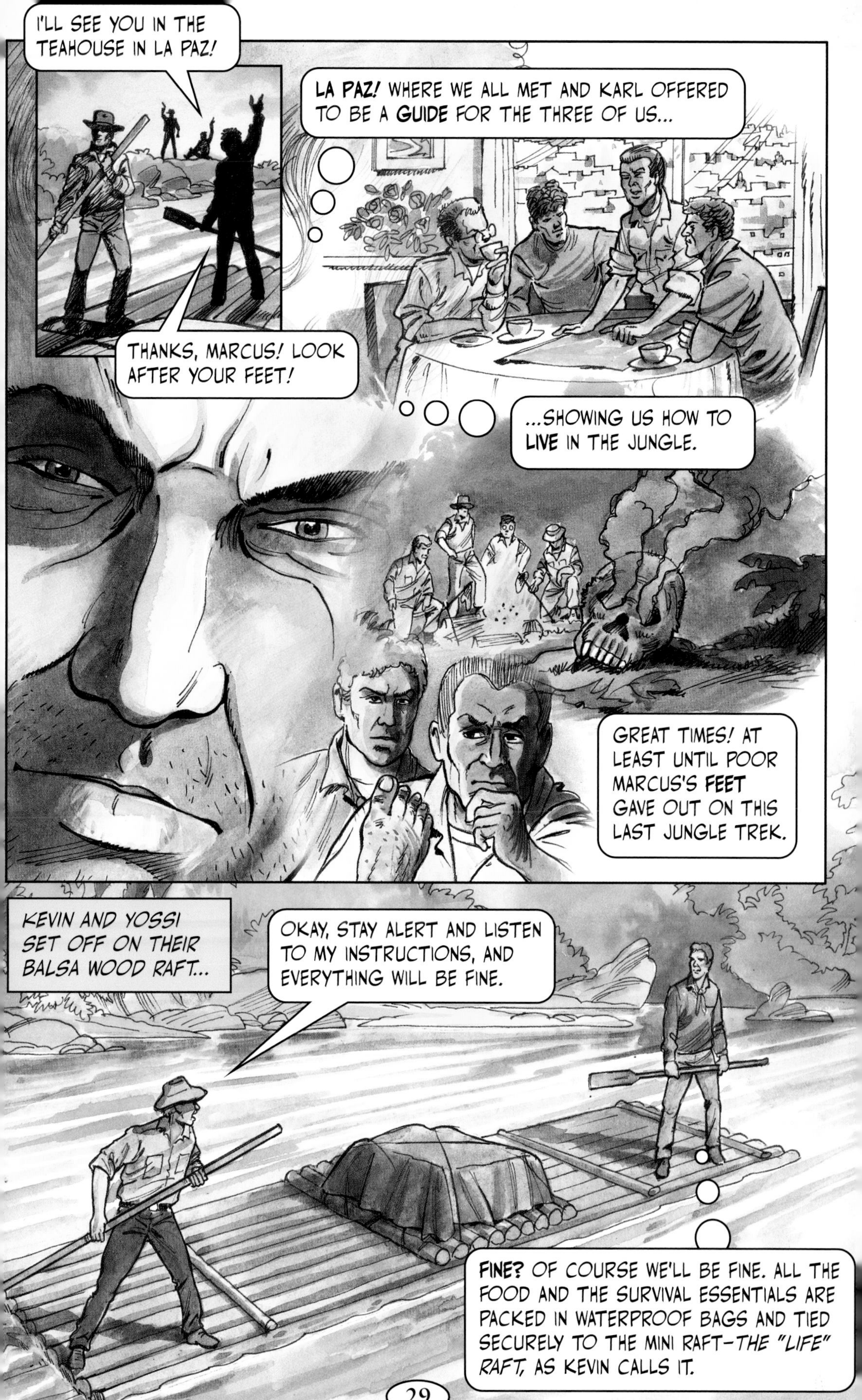
I'LL SEE YOU IN THE TEAHOUSE IN LA PAZ!
THANKS, MARCUS! LOOK AFTER YOUR FEET!
LA PAZ! WHERE WE ALL MET AND KARL OFFERED TO BE A GUIDE FOR THE THREE OF US...
...SHOWING US HOW TO LIVE IN THE JUNGLE.
GREAT TIMES! AT LEAST UNTIL POOR MARCUS'S FEET GAVE OUT ON THIS LAST JUNGLE TREK.
KEVIN AND YOSSI SET OFF ON THEIR BALSA WOOD RAFT...
OKAY, STAY ALERT AND LISTEN TO MY INSTRUCTIONS, AND EVERYTHING WILL BE FINE.
FINE? OF COURSE WE'LL BE FINE. ALL THE FOOD AND THE SURVIVAL ESSENTIALS ARE PACKED IN WATERPROOF BAGS AND TIED SECURELY TO THE MINI RAFT—THE "LIFE" RAFT, AS KEVIN CALLS IT.

THE RAPIDS ARE TOUGH...

PULL TO THE RIGHT!

THAT'S IT. WE'RE THROUGH! WE'LL REACH THAT SHORE KARL TOLD US ABOUT IN NO TIME!

THE SHORE! WHAT WAS IT KARL SAID...

"...WHEN YOU SEE THE SHORE, ROW HARD TO THE LEFT."

"YOU CAN'T MISS THE SHORE. IT'S OPPOSITE A BIG ISLAND WITH TALL TREES RIGHT IN THE MIDDLE OF THE RIVER. DITCH THE RAFT AND FOLLOW THE TRAIL TO SAN JOSE ON FOOT."

"WHATEVER YOU DO, DON'T GET PULLED INTO THE SAN PEDRO CANYON BEYOND."

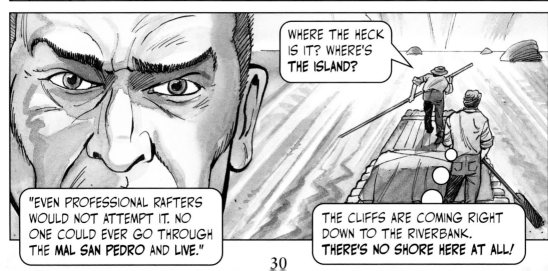

WHERE THE HECK IS IT? WHERE'S THE ISLAND?

"EVEN PROFESSIONAL RAFTERS WOULD NOT ATTEMPT IT. NO ONE COULD EVER GO THROUGH THE MAL SAN PEDRO AND LIVE."

THE CLIFFS ARE COMING RIGHT DOWN TO THE RIVERBANK. **THERE'S NO SHORE HERE AT ALL!**

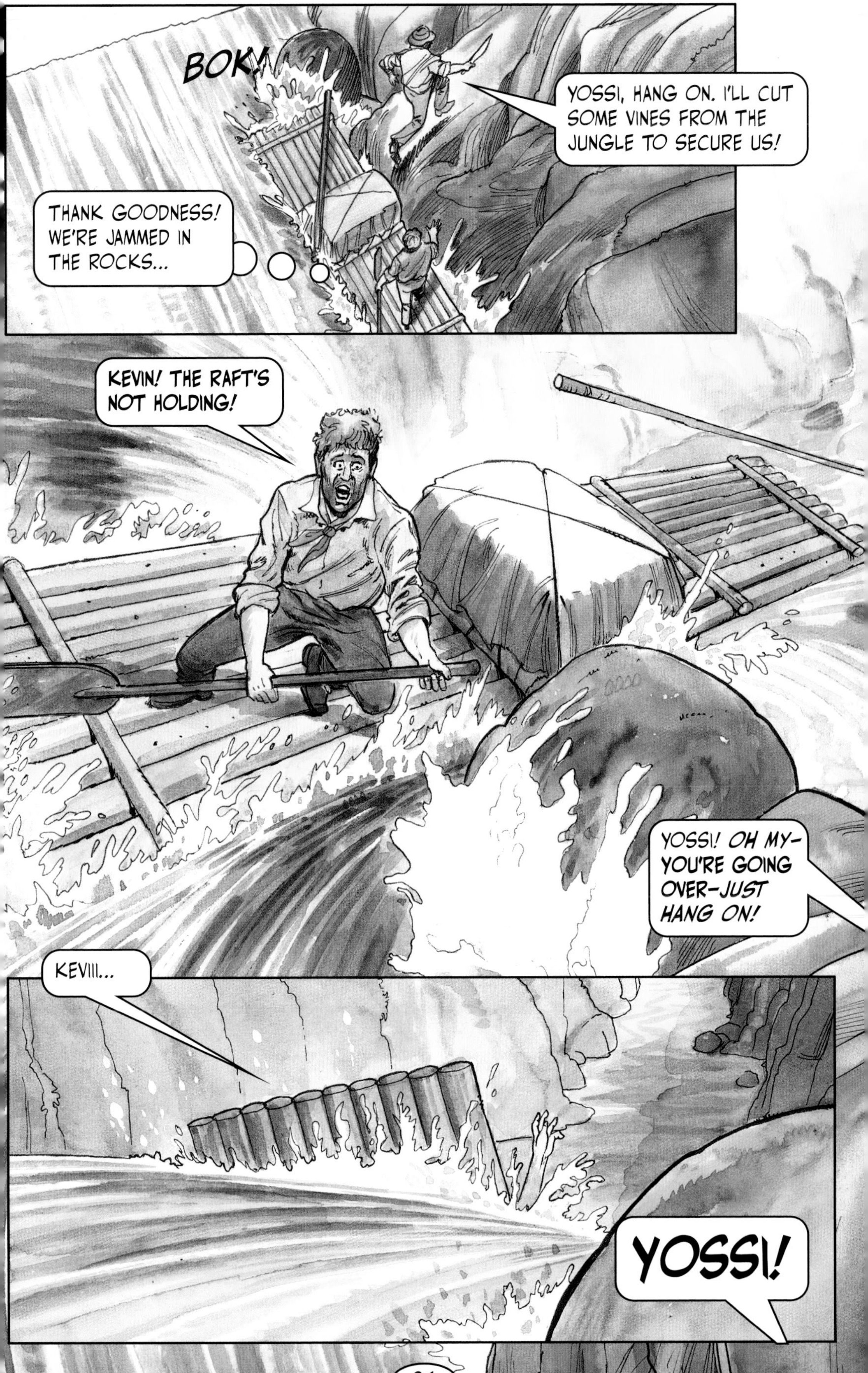
BOK!
YOSSI, HANG ON. I'LL CUT SOME VINES FROM THE JUNGLE TO SECURE US!
THANK GOODNESS! WE'RE JAMMED IN THE ROCKS...
KEVIN! THE RAFT'S NOT HOLDING!
YOSSI! OH MY- YOU'RE GOING OVER-JUST HANG ON!
KEVIII...
YOSSI!

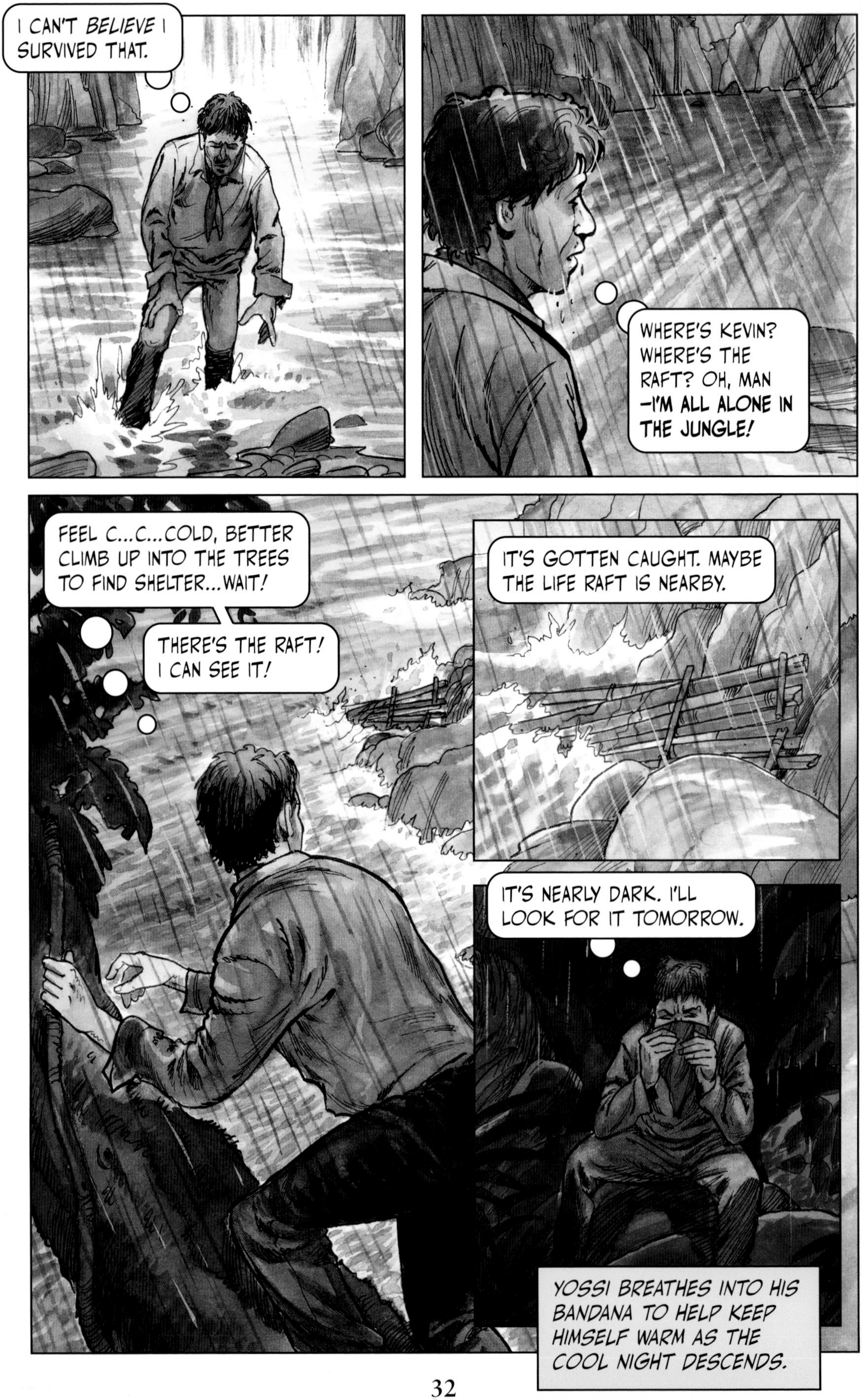
I CAN'T *BELIEVE* I SURVIVED THAT.
WHERE'S KEVIN? WHERE'S THE RAFT? OH, MAN —I'M ALL ALONE IN THE JUNGLE!
FEEL C...C...COLD, BETTER CLIMB UP INTO THE TREES TO FIND SHELTER...WAIT!
THERE'S THE RAFT! I CAN SEE IT!
IT'S GOTTEN CAUGHT. MAYBE THE LIFE RAFT IS NEARBY.
IT'S NEARLY DARK. I'LL LOOK FOR IT TOMORROW.
YOSSI BREATHES INTO HIS BANDANA TO HELP KEEP HIMSELF WARM AS THE COOL NIGHT DESCENDS.

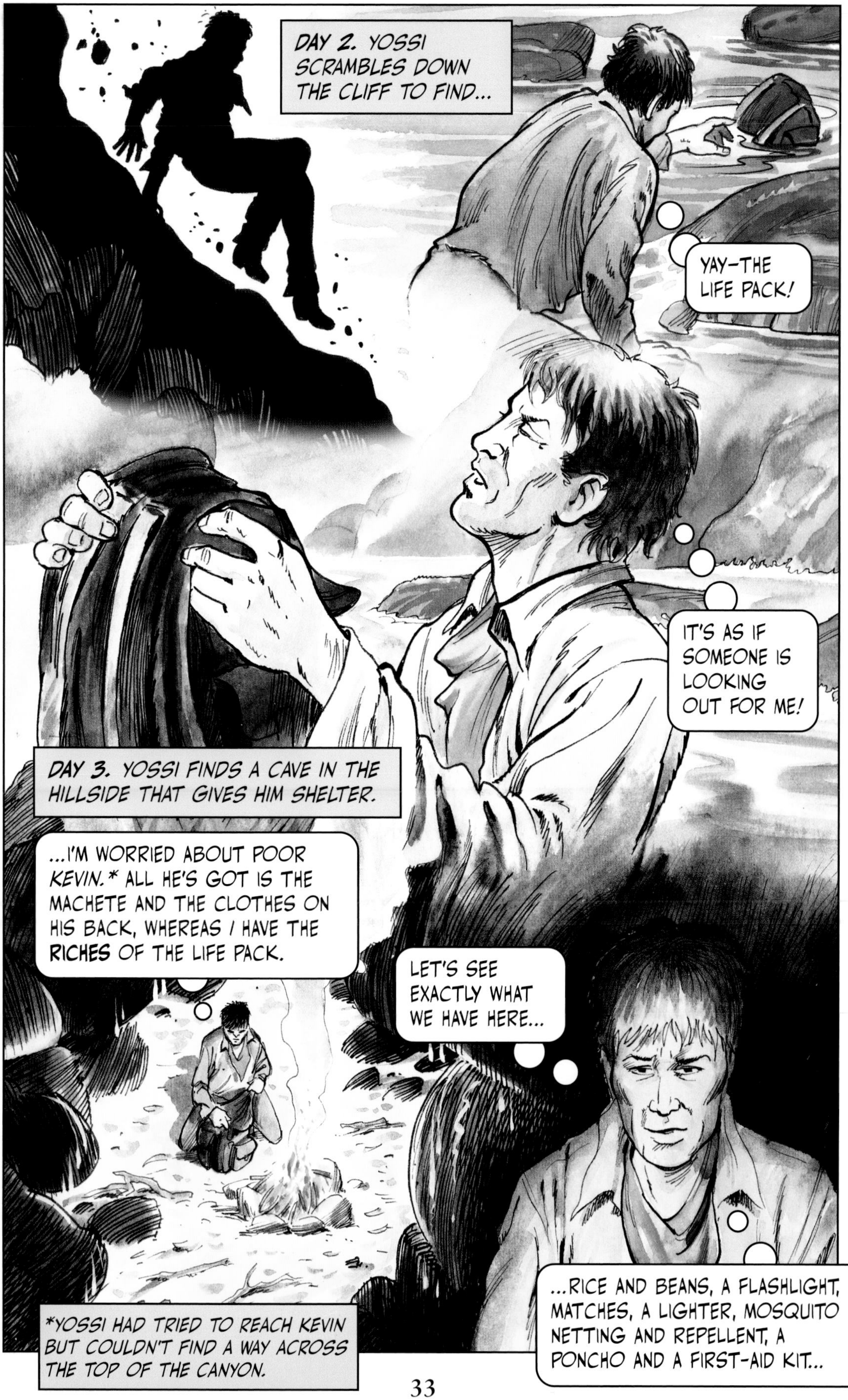
DAY 2. YOSSI SCRAMBLES DOWN THE CLIFF TO FIND...
YAY—THE LIFE PACK!
IT'S AS IF SOMEONE IS LOOKING OUT FOR ME!
DAY 3. YOSSI FINDS A CAVE IN THE HILLSIDE THAT GIVES HIM SHELTER.
...I'M WORRIED ABOUT POOR KEVIN.* ALL HE'S GOT IS THE MACHETE AND THE CLOTHES ON HIS BACK, WHEREAS I HAVE THE RICHES OF THE LIFE PACK.
LET'S SEE EXACTLY WHAT WE HAVE HERE...
...RICE AND BEANS, A FLASHLIGHT, MATCHES, A LIGHTER, MOSQUITO NETTING AND REPELLENT, A PONCHO AND A FIRST-AID KIT...
*YOSSI HAD TRIED TO REACH KEVIN BUT COULDN'T FIND A WAY ACROSS THE TOP OF THE CANYON.

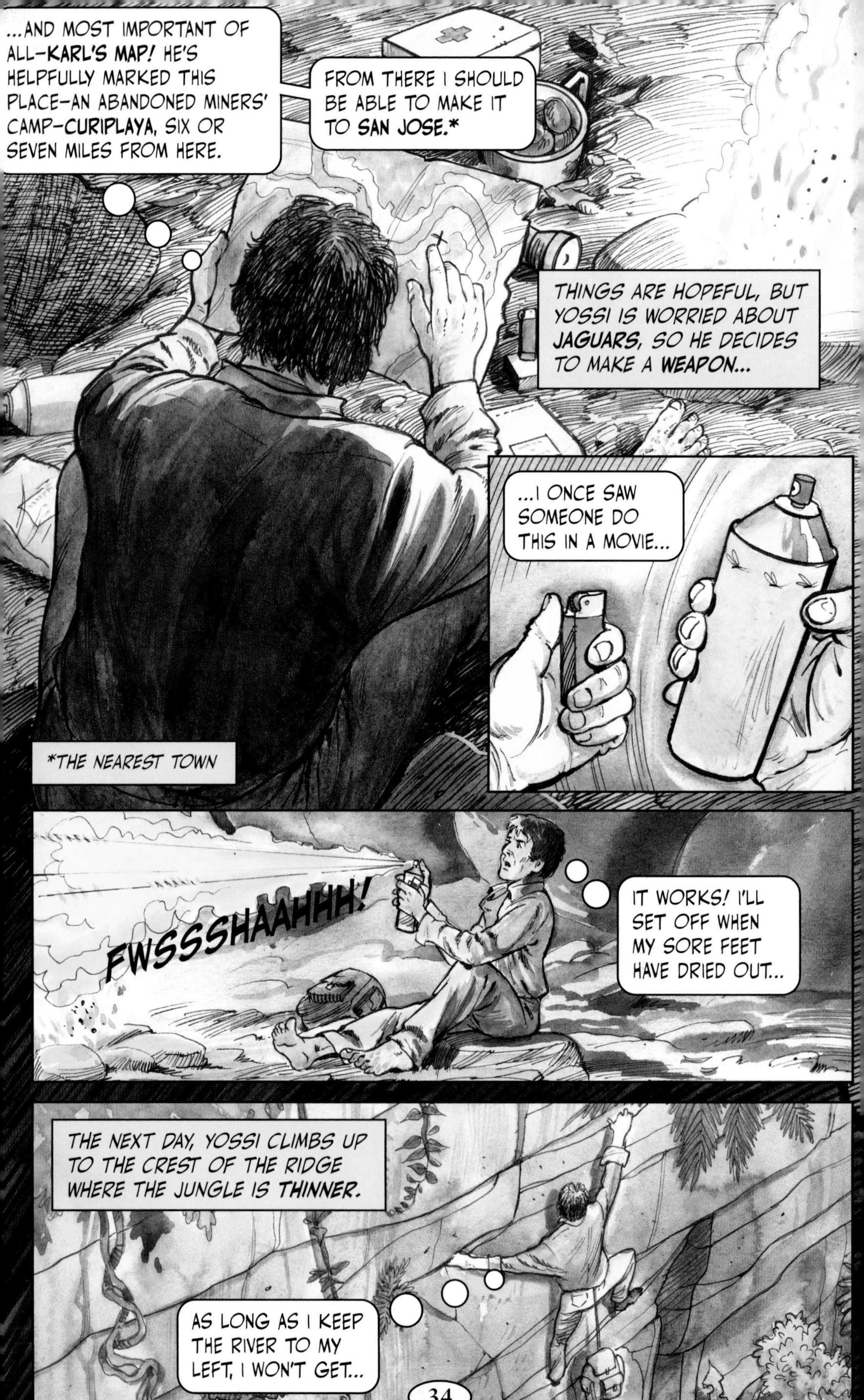
...AND MOST IMPORTANT OF ALL—KARL'S MAP! HE'S HELPFULLY MARKED THIS PLACE—AN ABANDONED MINERS' CAMP—CURIPLAYA, SIX OR SEVEN MILES FROM HERE.
FROM THERE I SHOULD BE ABLE TO MAKE IT TO SAN JOSE.*
THINGS ARE HOPEFUL, BUT YOSSI IS WORRIED ABOUT JAGUARS, SO HE DECIDES TO MAKE A WEAPON...
*THE NEAREST TOWN
...I ONCE SAW SOMEONE DO THIS IN A MOVIE...
FWSSSHAAHHH!
IT WORKS! I'LL SET OFF WHEN MY SORE FEET HAVE DRIED OUT...
THE NEXT DAY, YOSSI CLIMBS UP TO THE CREST OF THE RIDGE WHERE THE JUNGLE IS THINNER.
AS LONG AS I KEEP THE RIVER TO MY LEFT, I WON'T GET...

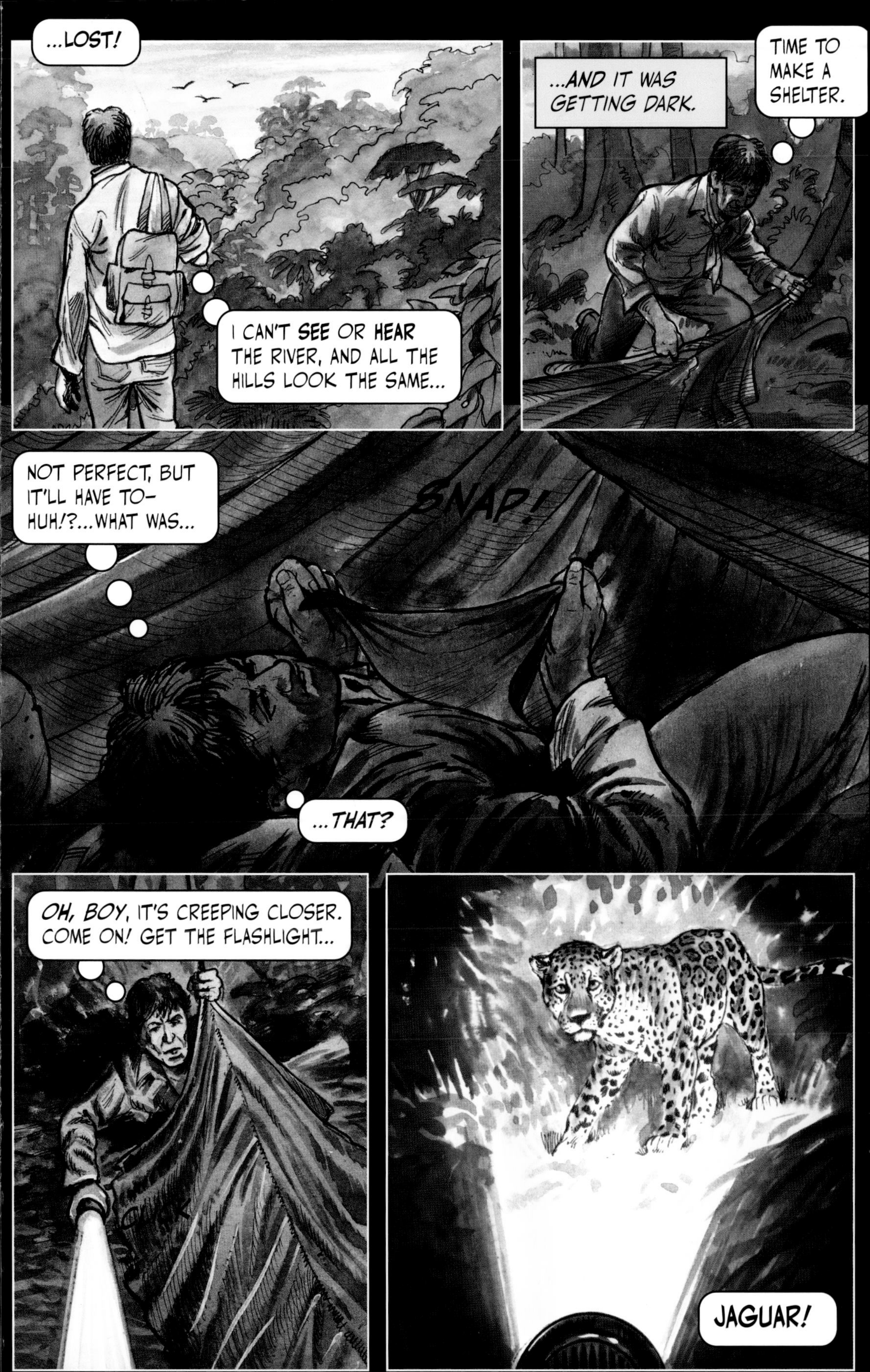
...LOST!
I CAN'T SEE OR HEAR THE RIVER, AND ALL THE HILLS LOOK THE SAME...
...AND IT WAS GETTING DARK.
TIME TO MAKE A SHELTER.
NOT PERFECT, BUT IT'LL HAVE TO– HUH!?...WHAT WAS...
SNAP!
...THAT?
OH, BOY, IT'S CREEPING CLOSER. COME ON! GET THE FLASHLIGHT...
JAGUAR!

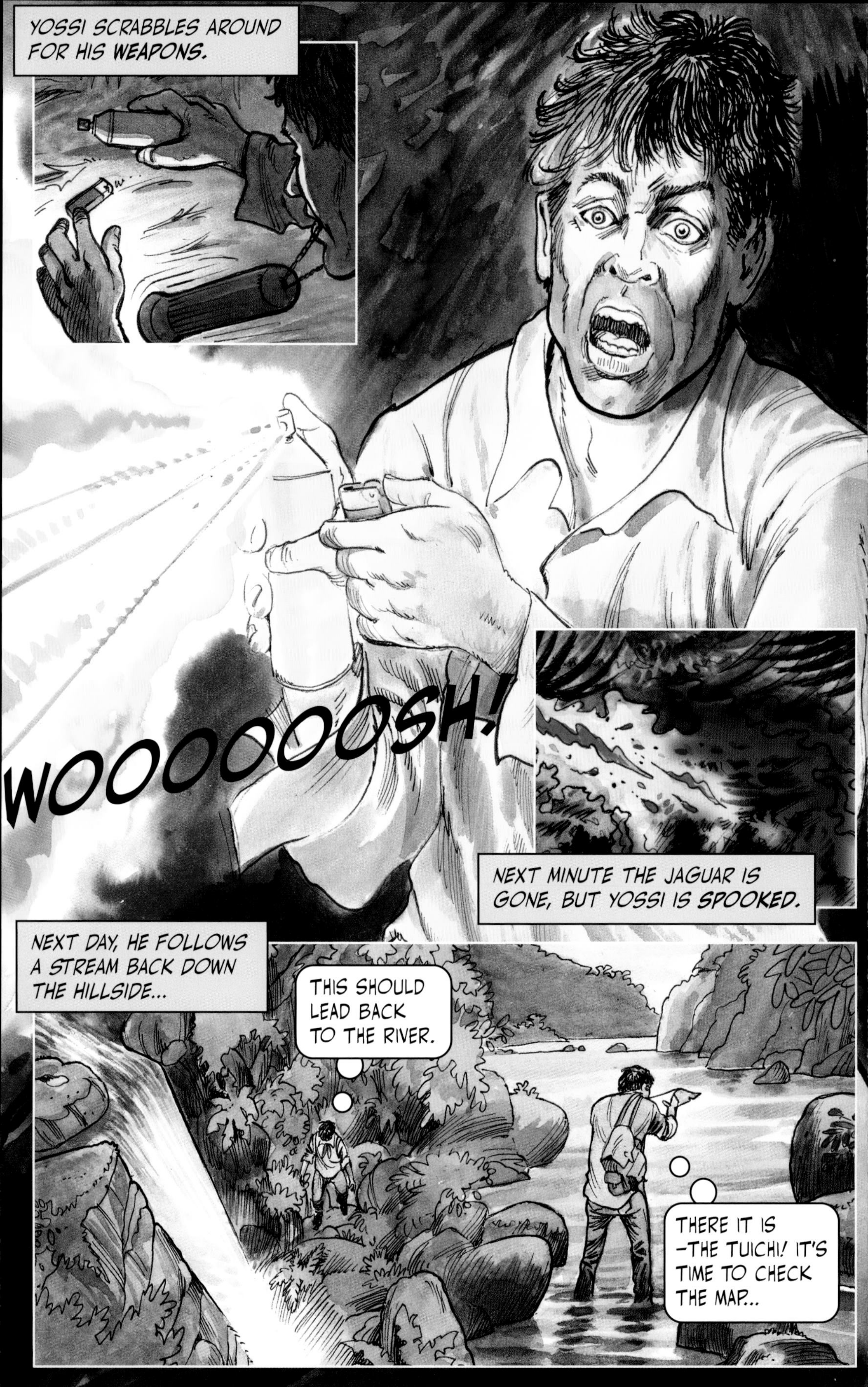
YOSSI SCRABBLES AROUND FOR HIS **WEAPONS.**
WOOOOOOOSH!
NEXT MINUTE THE JAGUAR IS GONE, BUT YOSSI IS **SPOOKED.**
NEXT DAY, HE FOLLOWS A STREAM BACK DOWN THE HILLSIDE...
THIS SHOULD LEAD BACK TO THE RIVER.
THERE IT IS –THE TUICHI! IT'S TIME TO CHECK THE MAP...

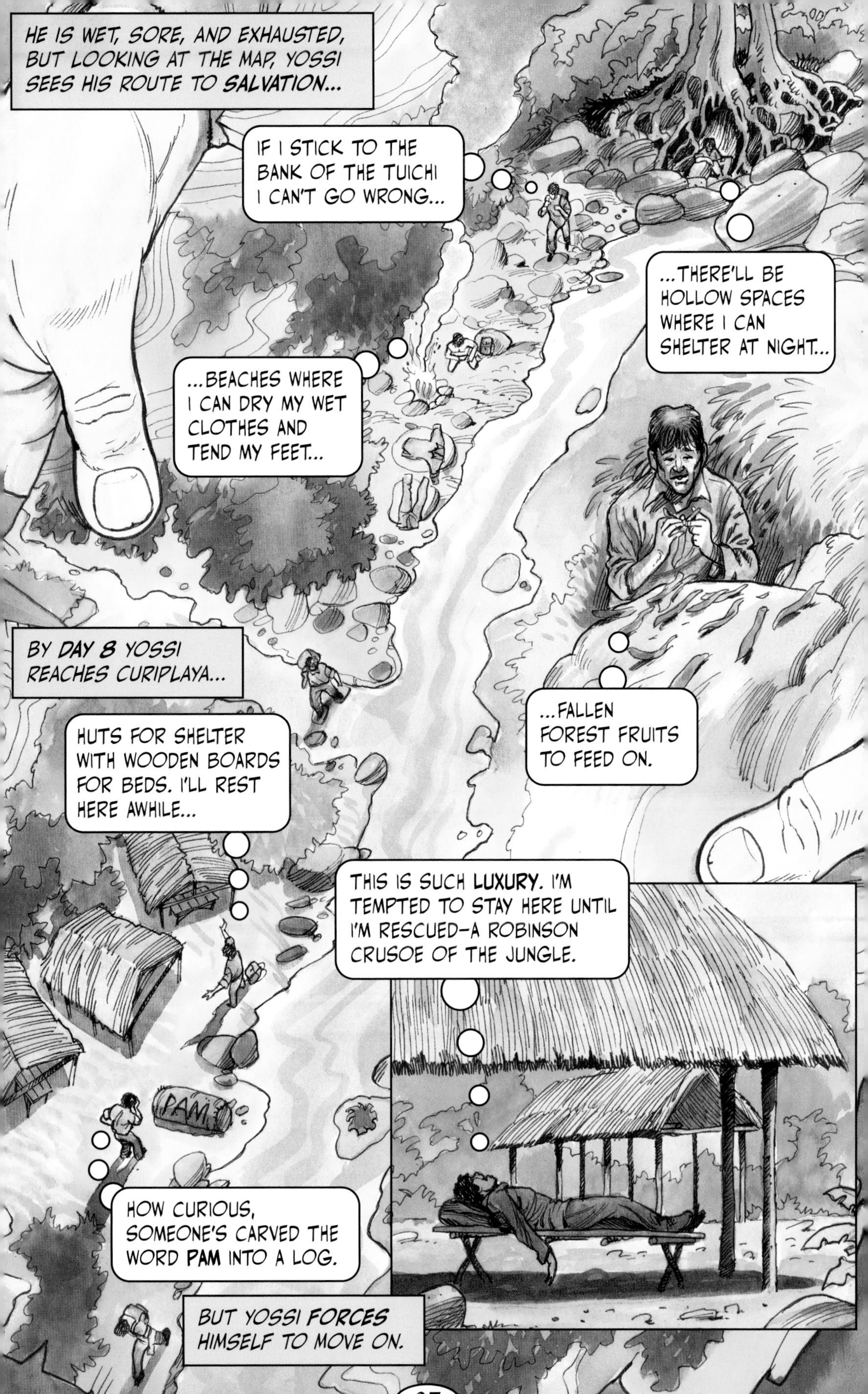
HE IS WET, SORE, AND EXHAUSTED, BUT LOOKING AT THE MAP, YOSSI SEES HIS ROUTE TO SALVATION...
IF I STICK TO THE BANK OF THE TUICHI I CAN'T GO WRONG...
...THERE'LL BE HOLLOW SPACES WHERE I CAN SHELTER AT NIGHT...
...BEACHES WHERE I CAN DRY MY WET CLOTHES AND TEND MY FEET...
...FALLEN FOREST FRUITS TO FEED ON.
BY DAY 8 YOSSI REACHES CURIPLAYA...
HUTS FOR SHELTER WITH WOODEN BOARDS FOR BEDS. I'LL REST HERE AWHILE...
THIS IS SUCH LUXURY. I'M TEMPTED TO STAY HERE UNTIL I'M RESCUED—A ROBINSON CRUSOE OF THE JUNGLE.
PAM
HOW CURIOUS, SOMEONE'S CARVED THE WORD PAM INTO A LOG.
BUT YOSSI FORCES HIMSELF TO MOVE ON.

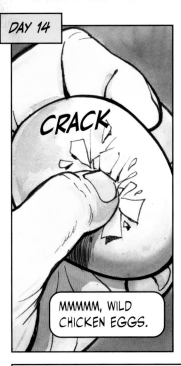

CRACK

MMMMM, WILD CHICKEN EGGS.

!

?...

SCOFF

I SHALL REMEMBER *THIS* PLACE AS **JAGUAR BEACH** BECAUSE OF ALL THE DROPPINGS AND FOOTPRINTS AROUND.

I WILL *ALSO* LEAVE MY *MARK*...

YOSSI LEAVES HIS INITIAL, THE DAY'S DATE, AND AN ARROW SHOWING HIS DIRECTION.

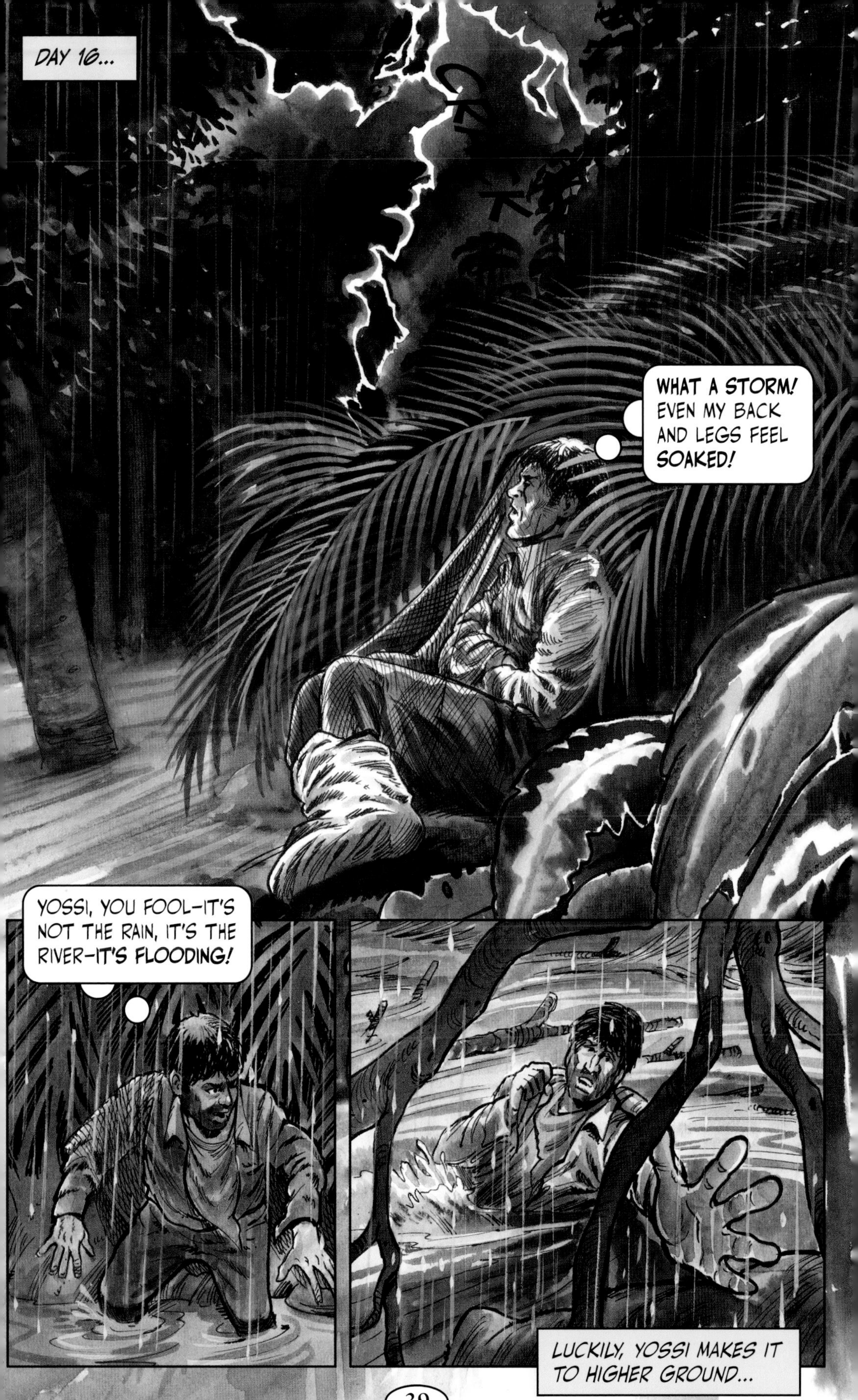
DAY 16...
WHAT A STORM! EVEN MY BACK AND LEGS FEEL SOAKED!
YOSSI, YOU FOOL–IT'S NOT THE RAIN, IT'S THE RIVER–IT'S FLOODING!
LUCKILY, YOSSI MAKES IT TO HIGHER GROUND...

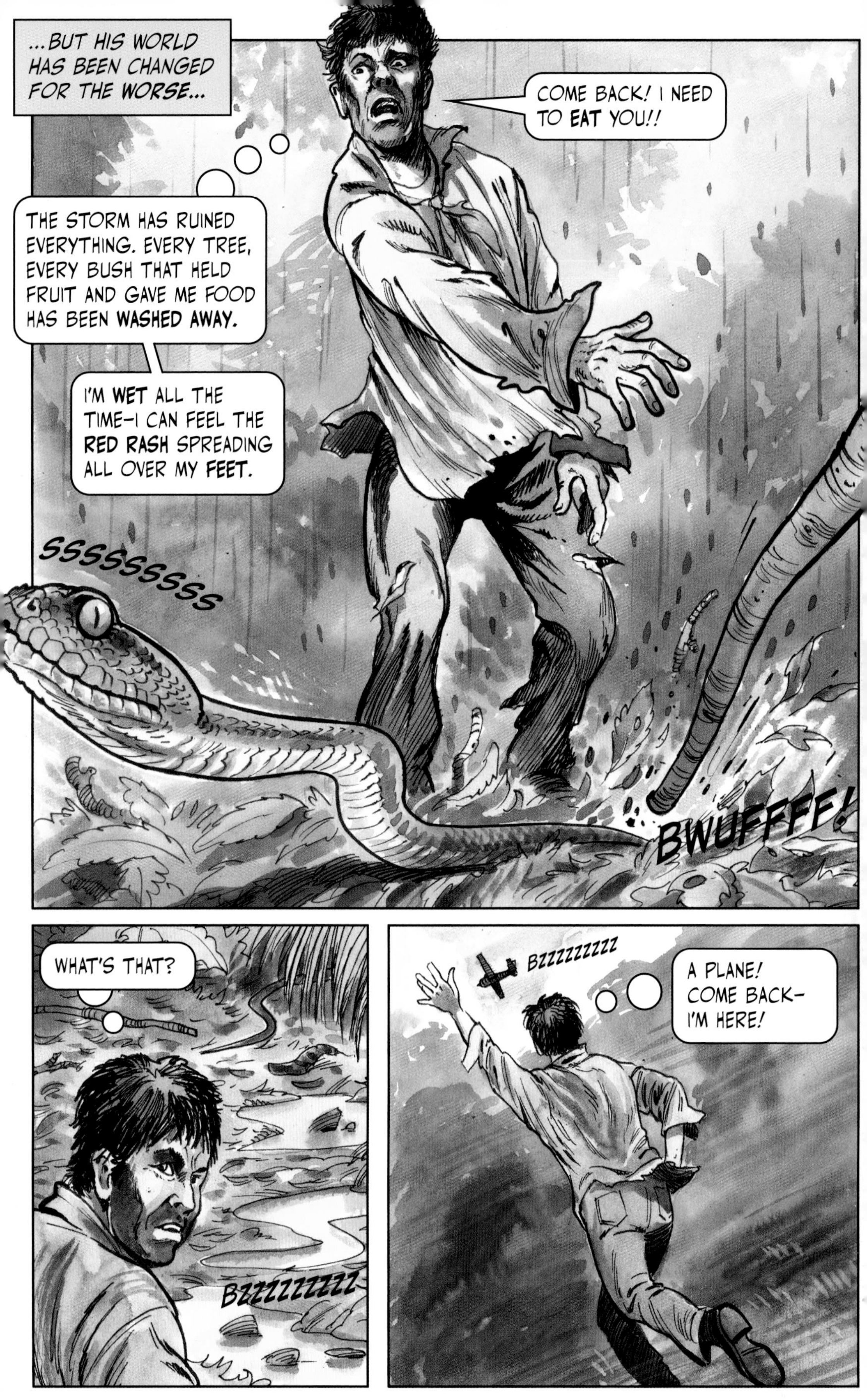
...BUT HIS WORLD HAS BEEN CHANGED FOR THE WORSE...
COME BACK! I NEED TO EAT YOU!!
THE STORM HAS RUINED EVERYTHING. EVERY TREE, EVERY BUSH THAT HELD FRUIT AND GAVE ME FOOD HAS BEEN WASHED AWAY.
I'M WET ALL THE TIME—I CAN FEEL THE RED RASH SPREADING ALL OVER MY FEET.
SSSSSSSSSS
BWUFFFFF!
WHAT'S THAT?
BZZZZZZZZZ
BZZZZZZZZZ
A PLANE! COME BACK— I'M HERE!

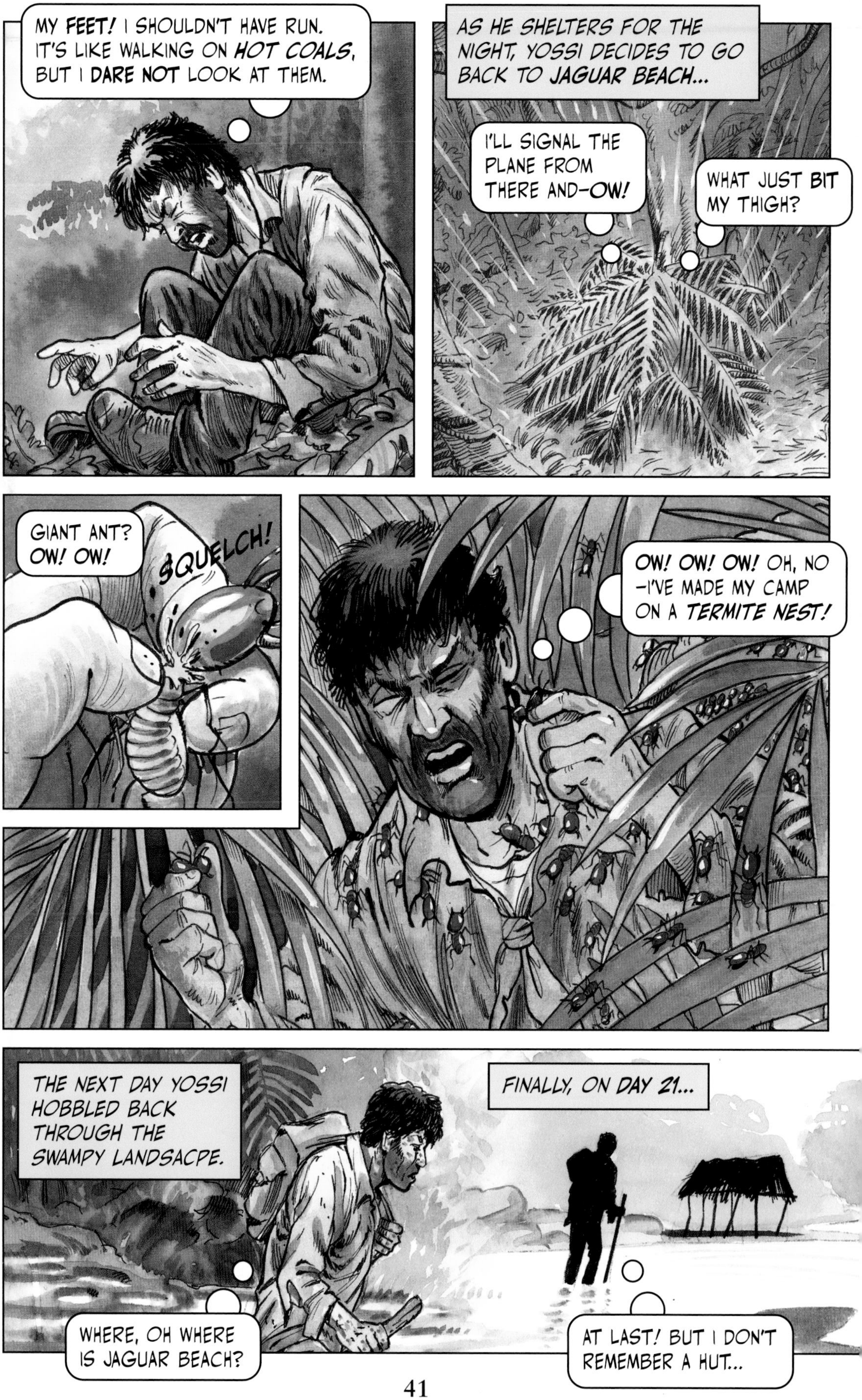
MY FEET! I SHOULDN'T HAVE RUN. IT'S LIKE WALKING ON HOT COALS, BUT I DARE NOT LOOK AT THEM.
AS HE SHELTERS FOR THE NIGHT, YOSSI DECIDES TO GO BACK TO JAGUAR BEACH...
I'LL SIGNAL THE PLANE FROM THERE AND—OW!
WHAT JUST BIT MY THIGH?
GIANT ANT? OW! OW!
SQUELCH!
OW! OW! OW! OH, NO —I'VE MADE MY CAMP ON A TERMITE NEST!
THE NEXT DAY YOSSI HOBBLED BACK THROUGH THE SWAMPY LANDSACPE.
WHERE, OH WHERE IS JAGUAR BEACH?
FINALLY, ON DAY 21...
AT LAST! BUT I DON'T REMEMBER A HUT...

...PAM? I'VE COME ALL THE WAY BACK TO *CURIPLAYA?!*

THE STORM HAD WASHED JAGUAR BEACH AWAY.

BUT YOSSI IS GLAD TO BE ABLE TO REST AND *FINALLY* REMOVE HIS SOCKS...

...NNNNYAAAAGHHH!

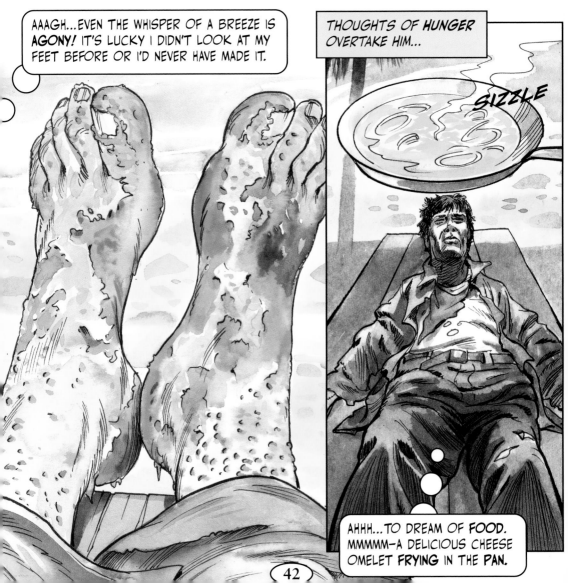

AAAGH...EVEN THE WHISPER OF A BREEZE IS *AGONY!* IT'S LUCKY I DIDN'T LOOK AT MY FEET BEFORE OR I'D NEVER HAVE MADE IT.

THOUGHTS OF *HUNGER* OVERTAKE HIM...

SIZZLE

AHHH...TO DREAM OF *FOOD.* MMMMM—A DELICIOUS CHEESE OMELET *FRYING* IN THE PAN.

YOSSI IS NEAR THE END...
WH...WHAT'S THAT NOISE...HELICOPTER?...
...PEOPLE?
PEOPLE!!
YOSSI?
KEVIN?
YOSSI, STAY THERE. I'M COMING!
YOSSI, THANK HEAVENS–I KNEW YOU WEREN'T DEAD!
KEVIN...KEVIN, YOU CAME BACK FOR ME!
KEVIN HAD MADE IT OUT ON DECEMBER 3 BY RIDING A LOG DOWN THE RIVER TO SAN JOSE. WHEN HE ASKED THE BOLIVIAN AUTHORITIES TO FIND YOSSI, THEY REFUSED, ARGUING THAT HIS FRIEND MUST ALREADY BE DEAD. USING MONEY FROM HOME, KEVIN CHARTERED A PLANE TO FLY OVER THE JUNGLE, BUT ALL TO NO AVAIL.
AS A LAST RESORT, KEVIN HAD HIRED SOME HUNTERS TO TAKE HIM UPRIVER FOR A FINAL SEARCH FOR HIS FRIEND.
THE END

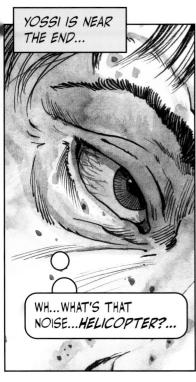

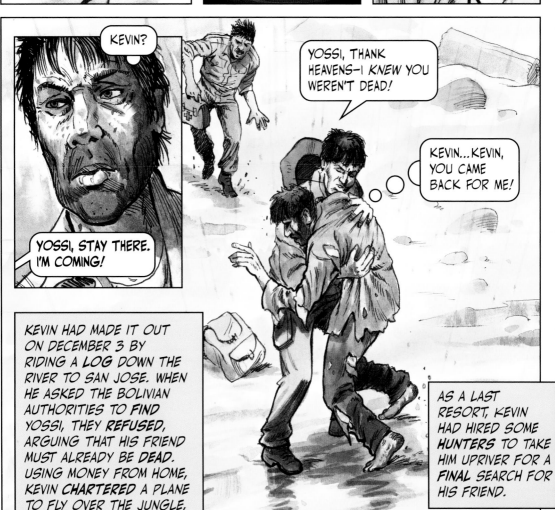

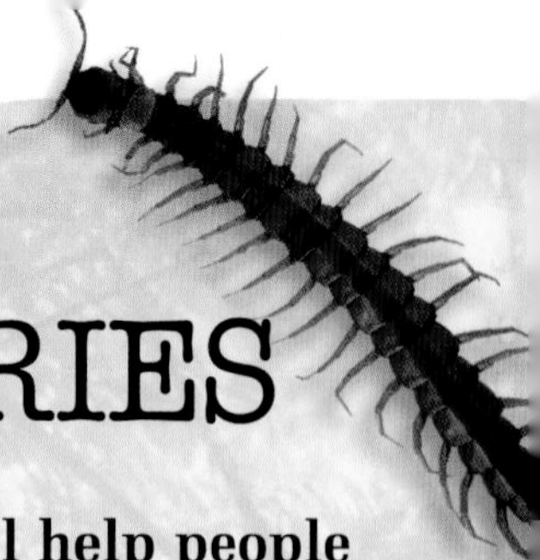

MORE JUNGLE SURVIVAL STORIES

Knowledge, training, and equipment can all help people manage in hostile jungle environments. But in a life or death situation survival often comes down to personal determination, and luck, as you will see...

STRANDED IN THE PERUVIAN JUNGLE, DECEMBER 24, 1971

On board LANSA Flight 508 out of Lima, 17-year-old German Juliane Koepcke gripped the seat arm tightly. The aircraft was bucking and twisting in the turbulence of a storm. Juliane cast a glance at her mother next to her. They had crossed the Andes and were heading for Pucallpa, deep in the Amazon rainforest.

Suddenly there was a blinding flash on the starboard wing. Panic engulfed the passengers as the plane dove vertically toward the ground. In the next instant the airplane disappeared from around Juliane, and she found herself free-falling, strapped to a row of three seats, two miles (three kilometers) above the jungle.

During the spiraling descent Juliane passed out. She awoke hours later, half buried under the seats, in mud on the rainforest floor. Amazingly, her only injuries were a swollen eye, cuts, and a broken collarbone. Her mother was gone. A huge rescue operation was mounted, but no one was found. The jungle seemed to have swallowed the plane and its 92 passengers whole.

Juliane, the daughter of a biologist who ran a field station in the jungle, knew that to survive she should follow a stream toward the river it fed. Suffering from a concussion, Juliane trekked through the dense jungle waterways for ten days, until she found an empty hut near a river.

Maggots had infested a wound on her arm, which she cleaned and dressed with items from the hut. Soon she was discovered by local lumbermen, who took her by canoe back to civilization. It was later discovered that as many as 14 other passengers also survived the initial fall from the shattered plane but were unable to seek help and died while awaiting rescue.

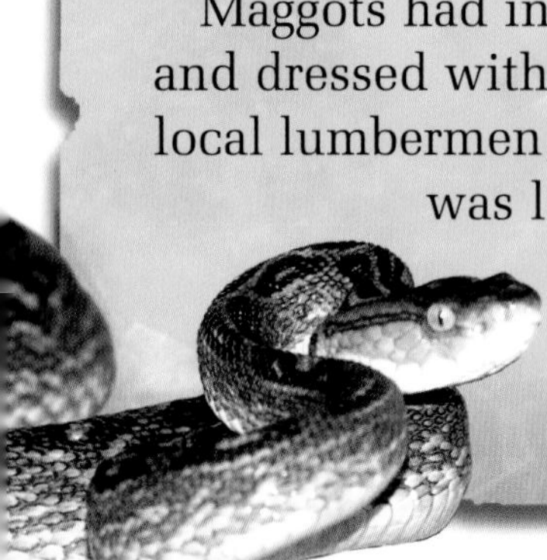

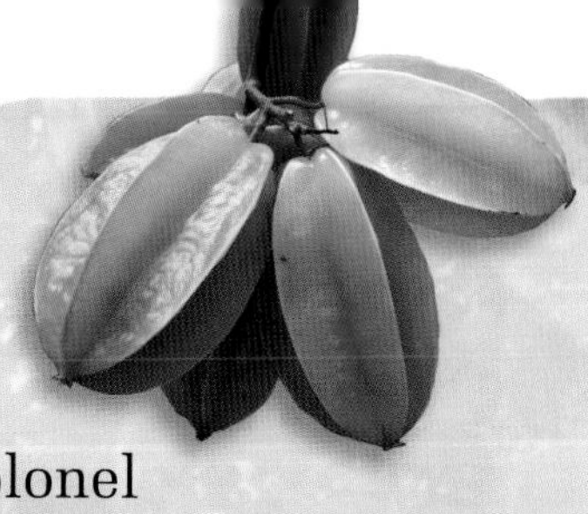

Trapped in Low's Gully, Borneo, March 1994

Low's Gully is a 1,000-foot (304 meter) abyss, carved by a glacier thousands of years ago, in the side of Mount Kinabalu. On February 22, 1994, ten soldiers, led by British Lieutenant-Colonel Robert Neill, began their descent to become the first to explore the unmapped depths of the mysterious canyon. After two exhausting days the team split into two groups. The fitter, more experienced mountaineers were going on ahead to complete the descent.

Colonel Neill was in the second group with a British major, Ron Foster, and three Chinese soldiers. The five stood on the brink of the final way down above the gully. With very few supplies left and the advance party far ahead of them, they had to decide whether to descend the gully or go back. They chose to go down.

After a hazardous descent, the five found themselves stranded in the bottom of the canyon, known locally as "the place of the dead." The advance party hadn't fared much better. Struggling through impossible terrain and with severe injuries, they reached civilization after 18 exhausting days and raised the alarm for the remaining five. Neill and his group were in dire straits. Their rations were running out and their morale was weakening by the day. They could do nothing but wait in the gully bottom. After three weeks they were rescued, on the verge of starvation.

Eaten by Lizards, Khammouane Province, Laos, July 2008

Forty-year-old Australian Hayden Adcock was hiking through Laos to Thailand. At a village he heard about a local waterfall and told the villagers he was setting off to find it. It was so impressive he decided to make the short trek onward to a second waterfall that he had heard about. Meanwhile it began to rain… hard.

The deluge washed away the path behind him. The misty, humid jungle yielded no clue about which way to go. Adcock became lost. The villagers searched for him but didn't know he'd gone to the second waterfall. He remained missing for 11 days before being spotted by an aerial search party.

Adcock had many superficial injuries, as well as blood poisoning and pneumonia. While he was unable to move for three days, lizards had stripped flesh from his legs, but he survived.

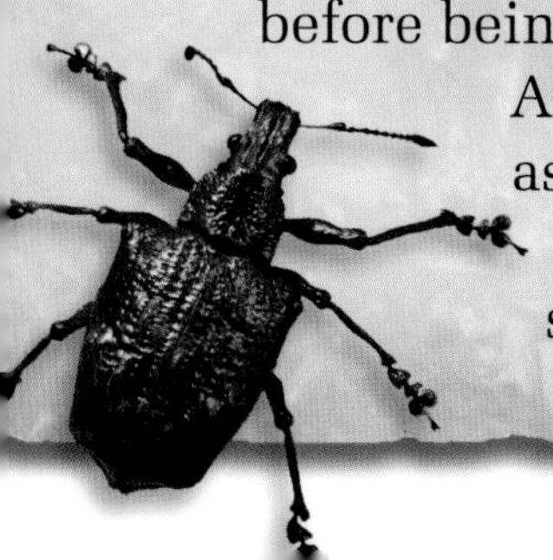

GLOSSARY

abundance A large supply.

balsa wood A very light, but very strong wood.

biodiversity The variety of life in a particular habitat or community of interacting organisms and their environment.

blowgun A long narrow pipe through which arrows, darts or stones can be blown.

canopy An overhanging shelter or shade.

chartered Rented, especially a plane or boat.

concussion Injury to the brain resulting from a trauma to the head, usually resulting in loss of consciousness.

dehydration To lose a large amount of water from the body.

disintegrates Breaks apart into tiny pieces.

equator The imaginary line that circles the Earth mid-way between the North and South Poles.

gully A deep ditch or channel cut in the earth by running water.

heatstroke Fever, and possibly unconsciousness, caused by failure of the body's temperature-regulating mechanism when exposed to excessive heat. Potentially fatal if left untreated.

humidity Atmospheric moisture.

machete A large heavy knife with a broad blade, used as a weapon and a tool for cutting vegetation.

malaria An infectious disease that can be transmitted by the bite of a mosquito.

palm hearts The soft, edible flesh inside the trunks of certain species of palm tree.

parasites Organisms that grow, feed and are sheltered on or in a different organism without helping their host's survival.

pneumonia A disease of the lungs that can cause difficulty in breathing.

rapids A fast-flowing part of a river, where the water is usually broken by rocks.

restraints Bindings that hold prisoners secure.

starboard The right-hand side of an aircraft or ship as one faces forward.

trekked Made a long exhausting journey.

vine A plant that needs support and climbs using tendrils, or creeps along the ground.

FOR MORE INFORMATION

ORGANIZATIONS

Rainforest Action Network
221 Pine Street, 5th Floor
San Francisco, CA 94104
USA
(202) 482-6090
Web site: http://ran.org/

The Rainforest Information Centre
Box 368
Lismore, NSW 2480
Australia
Web site: http://www.rainforestinfo.org.au/

FOR FURTHER READING

Albert, Toni. *The Remarkable Rainforest: An Active-Learning Book for Kids.* Mechanicsburg, PA: Trickle Creek Books, 2003.

Greenaway, Theresa. *Jungle (Eyewitness Books).* London, England: Dorling Kindersley, 2004.

Hogue Wojahn, Rebecca and Donald Wojahn. *A Rain Forest Food Chain: A Who-Eats-What Adventure in South America.* Minneapolis, MN: Lerner Publications, 2009.

Knight, Tim. *Journey into the Rainforest.* New York, NY: Oxford University Press, USA, 2001.

Mattern, Joanne. *Animals of the Tropical Rain Forest.* New York, NY: The Rosen Publishing Group, 2006.

INDEX

Web Sites

Due to the changing nature of Internet links, Rosen Publishing has developed an online list of Web sites related to the subject of this book. This site is updated regularly. Please use this link to access the list:

http://www.rosenlinks.com/ddss/jung/